HOME WINEMAKING FROM A TO Z

Also by Leo Zanelli

Shipwrecks Around Britain
Underwater Swimming—An Advanced Handbook

Home Winemaking from A to Z

by

Leo Zanelli

A. S. BARNES & CO.

NEW YORK AND SOUTH BRUNSWICK

First American edition published by
A. S. Barnes & Co., Inc.
Cranbury, NJ 08512
1972

Library of Congress Catalog Card No. 78-172516
ISBN 0-498-01062-7

All enquiries and requests relevant to this title should be
sent to the publisher at the above address, and not to
the printer.

Printed in the United States of America

To Marie, Mark and Craig
who help me empty the bottles

ERRATA

'Reisling' to read 'Riesling' throughout.

p 102, bottom line: '*Beutonite*' to read '*Bentonite*'.

p 106: Recipe for Rose Hip wine to read:
      'Fresh rose hips 3 lb *or* dried rose hips 12 oz'.

p 129: First line of 'Lychee' entry: 'decisious' to read
      'delicious'.

p 134: Recipe for Cowslip wine to read:
      'Water 1 gallon'.

Contents

Introduction

This book was not written with the intention of merely adding to the list of winemaking books available; it was built around three main principles that, in my opinion, are essential: Ease of Reference; Further Interest; and Pure Wines.

The first is simple to define and should apply to most books. It is for ease of reference that the main body consists of an alphabetical list.

A lack of further interest is where many hobbies or recreations founder. This is why I have tried to show that, apart from the more common home wines, commercial-type wines can also be attempted. And exotic wines. And even, if you have access to old books, wines of the type that were made hundreds of years ago. There is here a lifetime of experiment— and pleasant experiment at that.

Pure wine means just that. For instance, Apple wine should consist of—just apples. This may sound a strange statement, but there is a tendency for home winemakers to place a variety of ingredients in their brew and label it according to only one. For instance, if bilberries and raisins are the main ingredients it is usually called Bilberry wine, but it's not—it's really Bilberry and Raisin. Then again, a wine containing rose petals and grape concentrate will be called Rose wine, even though the concentrate will effectively mask the delicate taste and aroma of rose petals. The correct name, in this case, should be Grape and Rose Petal.

What I am getting at is the trend that automatically assumes that every home-made wine—whatever the basic fruit—should contain raisins, or grape concentrate or some other 'essential' ingredient. It is not that I am against these 'hybrid' wines, in fact my favourite is Bilberry and Raisin, but every wine-maker should first make the wine with a basic fruit and nothing else. Apple wine on its own can be magnificent. After experiment you may prefer to add sultanas or whatever. That's fine, but first make it from apple alone to see what real Apple wine is like.

That is the reason why all the recipes in this book, with the exception of Section 3, are devoted only to the ingredient titled.

Measurements

The recipes in this book have been presented in such a way that they may be used by both English and American winemakers without reference to conversion tables, in spite of the slight difference in measures that exist between the two countries. Very few of the recommended ingredients exceed 6 lb or 1 gallon, and for the purposes of winemaking the differences involved are so small that the resultant wines will be virtually identical.

For example, 4 lb of bilberries and a gallon of water using American measures will produce a wine almost indistinguishable from its English counterpart. To the expert, of course, the American wines will be slightly more full-bodied, but as the English prefer their wines lighter anyway, there will be no appreciable disadvantage to either.

Section One

Making wine   Why should we make wine? No doubt you already
have a fairly clear idea, or you would not be reading
this book, but there are many answers to the question.

Cost, is one. Making your own wine means that
you can drink wine at a price some 75 per cent or
more cheaper than what you would pay for the
commercially produced variety. This means that
you could, for instance, drink wine with virtually
every meal. A most civilized procedure!

Another reason could be that you don't like grape
wine! This may sound like heresy until a little
thought is given to it. After all, given two wines, one
made from grapes and the other from, say, bilberries,
which one would people prefer? Obviously some
would like the grape and some would prefer the
bilberry. In fact there are people who never liked
wine until they tasted some made from bilberry,
plum or whatever. They had found the wine they
preferred—and it wasn't grape. However, wine
made from other fruits is difficult, or impossible, to
buy and the obvious way is to make your own. Not
only that: while still on the subject of preference,
making your own wine means that you can evolve
a wine that suits you perfectly, with just the right
combination of sweetness, acidity and bite—in other
words, balanced to suit your individual palate. Try
ordering *that* from your wine merchant!

Then again, there is the satisfaction of producing
something you like, something of interest and value,
by means of your own personal skill. This alone
makes winemaking a worthwhile occupation to many
people.

Excellent wine—with suitable additions to make

up for natural deficiencies—can be made from virtually any fruit, vegetable or flower. It is even possible to produce a wine that compares favourably with commercial varieties, and this from such improbable ingredients as gooseberries, raisins and elderberries. The following pages will assist you but, although the answers to most of your questions will be found in Section Two, this in itself would serve no great purpose without a clear idea of how wine is made and of the procedure for making it at home. So let us examine what you will need, and how to go about it. First you will need some basic equipment.

Utensils The basic equipment for home winemaking is mostly very simple and you probably have some of it already. Wherever possible look up the appropriate part of Section Two (for instance, look up 'metal' before buying or using a metal boiling container).

Basic equipment:

Boiling container	At least 2 gallons capacity
Plastic pail	At least 2 gallons capacity
Glass fermentation jars	One gallon capacity
Air lock and bored bungs	One for each fermentation jar
Empty bottles	Wine bottles
Supply of bottle corks	
Plain bungs	To fit fermentation jars (for storing while the wine is clearing)
Nylon sieve	At least 6 inches diameter
Funnel	At least 6 inches diameter
Four feet of siphon tube	Rubber or plastic
Corking tool	You *could* bang the corks in with a flogger; but you'd be sorry!

| Hydrometer and trial jar | Not essential, but you must have one if you want consistent results |

That should take care of your initial efforts. Later on you may acquire refinements such as a press, larger fermentation jars and so on, but for the present the list given should suffice.

Ingredients   Next you will require certain ingredients for adding to the wine 'must'. Some are essential, some are merely for flavour or balance. Once again, this list is for your initial efforts. You may never use any more.

Basic ingredients:

Yeast	Bakers' yeast will do at a pinch, but try to lay in a supply of wine yeasts. If you want only one type in stock, make it the All Purpose.
Yeast nutrient	Sold as such. This provides 'food' for the yeast.
Campden tablets	For sterilizing and inhibiting mould growth.
Citric acid	About $\frac{1}{4}$ lb.
Tannin	A small tube. Grape tannin is best, but not essential.
Depectinizer	Small packet. Also known as Pectic Enzyme.
Sugar	Ordinary table sugar. You will need approximately 3 lb for each gallon of wine made.

Making a wine   In the field of learning or teaching there is still nothing better than practical experience. Ideally we should make a batch of wine together. This is obviously impossible—but we can do a literary run through a batch of wine. If you have the ingredients you can try out the procedure at home now. But read through this section first, preferably several times. We will run through the procedure using the

recipe for my favourite red wine. Get the following
ingredients:

Bilberry and Raisin wine (dry)
Dried bilberries   ¾ lb
　　　or
Fresh bilberries   4 lb
Minced raisins   ¼ lb
Sugar   2 lb
Citric acid   teaspoon
Yeast: Burgundy
Yeast nutrient
Water   1 gallon

Place the bilberries, raisins and sugar in a plastic
pail. Bring the water to the boil and pour (boiling)
over the fruit and sugar. Allow to cool. Keep the pail
well covered with a cloth.

When cool, add the citric acid, yeast and yeast
nutrient. The pail must be kept covered at all times.

At this stage you will have a dark red liquid with
the fruit residing firmly at the bottom. After a few
days (or earlier if you have used a 'starter') the fruit
will have risen to the surface, forming what is called
the 'cap'. Your wine is now fermenting.

Stir daily, breaking the cap up well. Allow
fermentation to continue in the covered pail for five
days.

At the end of this period, strain the liquid into a
fermentation jar by means of the nylon strainer and
funnel. Fit an air lock and watch the bubbles easing
through. Wine is being made!

The bubbles will, initially, gurgle through the
liquid in the air lock at a fairly fast rate. After a few
days they will slow down. The process of fermentation
will take several weeks in relatively warm weather.
In cooler weather it might take many months.

When the bubbles no longer occur, and the water
in the air lock has levelled off, taste the wine for

sweetness. If fermentation has been complete there should be no trace of sugar.

Racking

Your wine will now be a rather cloudy liquid that probably, at this stage, won't even taste nice. Remove the air lock and replace it with a bung. After a week or two it can be racked off the bottom sediment.

To rack, place the fermentation jar containing the wine on a table and another, empty, fermentation jar on the floor. Insert the siphon tube into the wine in the top jar, keeping it well clear of the bottom sediment. The other end of the tube is then lowered to a point lower than the bottom of the wine; place the siphon tube in your mouth—and suck. When the wine is flowing the tube is placed into the neck of the lower, empty jar, and the wine is racked off the sediment. When this has been done, recork the jar containing the wine and put it away to clear.

If you are worried about the hygiene aspect of placing the siphon tube in your mouth, there are special tubes made with a manual pump on the end.

Clearing

Clearing is a variable. Some wines become crystal clear in a few days, others take weeks, months—or never, unless assisted. The last mentioned have to be assisted by means of filtration, or fining. Until recently the commercial winemaker had virtually only one really complete advantage over the amateur —the commercial filter devices that enable the producers to filter vast amounts of wine to render it stable and clear. These filters were not available in a unit small enough to be economic or feasible. However, there are now at least two small units available to the amateur, both at a reasonable price. With these units a technological revolution is taking place in filtration methods. In fact it is my personal conviction that these new units—and the models that will follow them—will set standards of clarity that will make all existing methods obsolete.

Fermentation

To continue the exercise, let's go back over the batch of wine you have just 'produced'. First, the fermentation.

Two essentials are necessary for fermentation to take place, and without the fermentation there is no alcohol—or wine. This requires, basically, yeast and sugar. When present in a liquid the yeast, if the temperature is suitable (78°F or 25°C to start it off), will start to feed on the sugar and, as a result, produce an approximate 50–50 combination of carbon dioxide, which vanishes into the atmosphere via the air lock, and alcohol (which we strive to keep!). During this period if the temperature gets too low (under 50°F or 10°C) the fermentation will slow down or stop. If it becomes too high (over 90°F or 38°C) the yeast will die.

The yeast will go on feeding on the sugar and producing alcohol until (*a*) the sugar supply is exhausted, in which case you will end up with a dry wine (unless you add more sugar) or (*b*) the concentration of alcohol becomes so high that it kills the yeast. When this happens, and sugar remains, the wine will be sweet.

Yeast and alcohol tolerance

You may have noticed that I referred to the possibility of alcohol killing the yeast. This is a scientific fact, so dismiss the stories of Aunt Maud making wine that is as strong as whisky—it just can't be done unless you add alcohol artificially. With a good strain of yeast and good technique you might be able to make a wine that contains about 20 per cent alcohol by volume, and that's the limit.

But then, we don't require a table wine even as strong as that, because 20 per cent is the strength of Port and Sherry and much too strong to drink during a meal.

Yeast nutrient and acid

This is often known as yeast food. There are ingredients needed for the yeast to act efficiently and one of them is phosphate. Don't be frightened by the pharmaceutical-sounding name. It is sold in winemaking shops as yeast nutrient and is very simple to use.

Another ingredient often labelled as a yeast food is acid—citric, tartaric or malic. Some people consider that acid is essential for yeast growth. This is not strictly true. But acid *is* required if the wine is to be well balanced; while grapes, for instance, usually have enough, fruits such as dessert cherries and elderberries have too little and need some acid added, whereas fruit such as grapefruit usually have too much and need to be diluted.

Sulphiting Probably the most serious winemaking problem is bacterial infection. To this effect sulphur has been used for hundreds of years as a means of keeping a wine free from such problems.

Some winemakers will not touch any such addition, but most do and there is no doubt that it helps produce good wine more easily and perhaps consistently. The modern winemaker achieves this by adding one crushed Campden tablet to each gallon of wine 'must' at the start. I would personally recommend the procedure, but it is really a matter of personal preference.

In any case, the important point to note is that when some form of sterilant such as Campden is used, the 'must' should be left at least twenty-four hours before introducing the yeast because the sulphite has an inhibiting effect on yeast.

Pectin Another serious problem that can occur is a pectin haze. Some ingredients such as dried apricots are inclined to exude a substance which will make a wine permanently cloudy. To eliminate this a depectinizer (sold as Pectolitic Enzyme) is added to the must. This has the effect of destroying the haze substance at an early stage.

Depectinizer, like Campden, has an inhibiting effect on yeast so, if it is used, at least twenty-four hours must elapse before the yeast is introduced.

Other wines There are several other ways in which we could have made our wine if other ingredients had been used. For instance, if we had used a delicate ingredient such as flower heads, they would have been soaked in cold water to extract the taste (boiling water would have destroyed the delicate flavour). If we had used apples they would have been crushed or chopped with boiling water poured over them. Dried fruit would invariably have been washed, chopped, placed in water and brought to the boil before cooling and proceeding.

Bacteria and cleanliness

Bacterial infection turning wine into vinegar, or some other dread malady, is something one must always be on guard against. This means that all apparatus, bottles and corks must be scrupulously clean—and so should the wine must. This means sterilizing the fruit or must by means of boiling or chemical additions. Some people will never boil the must because, they say, it spoils the flavour, and to a certain extent it can do so with some ingredients. Others simply will not use chemicals at any price. Both points of view are misguided. Ingredients such as elderberries and raisins suffer little—if at all—by being immersed in boiling water. The point is, nothing should be actually boiled in water. The ingredients are placed in cold water and brought to the boil. There are a few ingredients that will not suffer through being boiled for several minutes, but not many.

On the other hand, flower wines are destroyed by boiling water, and soaking in cold water leaves the must seriously open to infection. In this case it is wise to sulphite by means of one Campden tablet to each gallon of must.

Methods of winemaking

Although there are a number of variations of a subtle nature, there are really three main ways of making wine. For convenience and to save space I have called them methods A, B and C. Any small additions or alterations will be inserted under the specific recipe.

Before you take note of the methods, run over the following observations. Some of them are 'repeats' because they are so important.

Whenever using Campden tablets or depectinizer in the must, always allow twenty-four hours before introducing the yeast.

Quantities of ingredients such as flowers are used with liquid measures, e.g. 1 gallon of flower heads means a one-gallon measure, such as a pail, filled level with flower heads.

Whenever possible, introduce the yeast as a 'starter' (see Section 2).

The basic method

1. Ensure that the ingredients and quantities are correct.
2. Make up the must.
3. If necessary add a Campden tablet or depectinizer at this stage (if added, leave for twenty-four hours).
4. Add remaining ingredients, except for yeast.
5. Initiate fermentation by adding yeast, preferably by using a 'starter bottle'.
6. When the ingredients have been in the must for the specified time, strain into a fermentation jar and fit an air lock.
7. When the fermentation has finished, rack the wine off into another jar leaving the yeast sediment, or lees, behind. At this stage a stabilizer can be added if required.
8. If the wine does not clear within six weeks it can be racked again, fined or filtered with one of the units on the market. The latter is certainly the most convenient procedure.
9. When the wine is crystal clear, taste it. It will probably taste horrible! It should now be bottled and you can use your initial 'tasting' as a guide. If it really did taste horrible, leave the wine several months before drinking. If it tasted nice, well, it's up to you!

Making the must is where the most deviation occurs, so the following methods are used throughout the book.

Method A

Bring the water to the boil, adding the sugar.
Allow to cool.
Add the main ingredients along with Campden or depectinizer if required.
Add all other ingredients except yeast.
Introduce yeast or starter.
When the must is fermenting leave in a container covered with a cloth in 'aerobic' fermentation for the number of days indicated in the recipe.
Strain off into fermentation jar and fit air lock.

Method B

Place the main ingredient and the sugar in a container.
Pour boiling water over and stir.
Allow to cool.
Continue as for method A.

Method C

Place the main ingredient and the sugar in a metal container and bring to the boil.
Allow to cool.
Continue as for method A.

The most usual source of confusion and danger is during the aerobic fermentation. It is not strictly necessary to allow unlimited air to the must. In fact this part of the procedure is really to allow the must to absorb the colour and flavour of the main ingredients. To this extent it is quite permissible, indeed desirable, to limit the invasion of bacteria. A sheet of towelling stretched over the container over which is placed a flat board or lid is a suitable procedure. Or you can get a large plastic bag, place the container in it, gather the opening around the handle of a long spoon or other stirring device and tape the plastic opening round the handle. The liquid can then be stirred daily without the danger of organisms invading the must.

Finally, if available always use a hydrometer. And before you use any ingredient, utensil or technique (e.g. yeast, hydrometer, racking), refer to it in Section Two.

Section Two
A–Z

An alphabetical list of home winemaking recipes, equipment, ingredients, terms and techniques

Acetaldehyde Part of the process in which enzymes convert sugar into alcohol. The action of enzymes does this in five stages; at the fourth stage the enzyme carboxylase forms acetaldehyde and carbon dioxide from pyruvic acid. At the next and final stage acetaldehyde is reduced to ethyl alcohol, but a minute quantity remains and adds to the flavour of the wine.

Acetobacter Aerobic bacteria which has the property of using oxygen present in the air to convert some of the wine alcohol primarily to acetaldehyde, then to acetic acid (vinegar). Air is essential for its growth, and this is one of the reasons why storage containers should be kept topped up and the air spaces in bottles kept to a minimum.

Acid, Acetic Formed by the action of the bacteria acetobacter, turning the wine to vinegar.

Acid, Ascorbic This is vitamin C and is used, like Campden tablets, as an antoxidant by preventing wine from taking up air and oxidizing.

Acid, Butyric A 'spoiling' acid cauxed by micro-infection.

Acid, Citric Present in many fruits in varying quantities, citric is the most commonly used acid additive in home wine production. It has the advantage over tartaric acid in that it is less harsh to the taste and does not give deposits of crystals. Some fruits, such as lemon, have an excess of acid, as do grapefruit and orange. In these cases it is necessary to dilute the juice with water. On the other hand, vegetables and cereals have little or no acid and something like $\frac{1}{2}-\frac{3}{4}$ oz to the gallon needs to be added.

Acid, Ellagic One of the tannins which are present in the skins and seeds of fruit and which, in quantity, gives a wine an astringent taste.

Acid, Galacturonic	Part of the chemical composition of pectin.
Acid, Glyceric	A product of the process by which enzymes convert sugar into alcohol. In this case triose is converted into glycerine and glyceric acid.
Acid, Lactic	A bacterial infection of an anaerobic nature produces lactic acid by breaking down tartaric acid or malic acid. Lactic acid has a rather sour flavour, but can add to the smoothness of a wine, so it is often encouraged in small quantities. Sugars and nitrogen nutrients favour the growth of the bacteria and for this reason it is not wise to let the wine stand on the lees after fermentation.
Acid, Malic	Present in many fruits, malic can be converted into lactic acid if it undergoes a malolactic fermentation. For this reason it requires careful use. Where malic acid is used in wine production an ample amount of sulphur dioxide should be included as this chemical actively inhibits malolactic fermentation; however, striking the correct balance between the proportions of malic acid and sulphur dioxide is not a job for the amateur.
Acid, Propionic	One of the 'spoiling' acids which occur as the result of bacterial infection.
Acid, Succinic	An acid which is extremely resistant to bacterial attack and which always occurs in alcoholic fermentation.
Acid, Tartaric	The acid of the grape. Sometimes used in place of citric acid in wine must. It has a somewhat harsher taste, but this is preferred by some. If any potassium or calcium is present in the wine, tartaric acid can combine with either of these to form cream of tartar or calcium tartrate. If this happens the wine will give off small deposits of crystals, particularly if exposed to sudden cold.
Acid, Volatile	A name which covers most of the 'spoiling' acids, including acetic, propionic and butyric.
Acidity	All wine has a certain amount of acid. If the wine can be described as acid, it has too much. On the

other hand, if it contains too little it will be flat and insipid. There is also the acidity of natural tartaric and malic acid, which in excess is described as 'tart'; or a spoiled wine tasting of vinegar, which means the wine is sour and is almost always evidence of poor or careless production technique or storing.

It is generally thought that acidity is required for yeast growth, but this is not strictly true. However, acidity is required if the wine is to have good balance, keeping qualities and resistance to infection. Where juice such as grapefruit is being used, acid will be in excess and the juice will have to be diluted with water; however, some fruits and vegetables contain too little and will need the addition of some acid—usually citric—to the must.

Additives   The collective name used for a group of products which, while not essential to the production of wine, can be added to improve the wine or ease its production; it includes depectinizing enzymes, yeast foods, etc.

Aerobic   Quite literally means 'exposed to air'. When fruit is fermenting, initially, in a pail/barrel/container with only a covering cloth to keep off insects, it is exposed to air and is said to be in aerobic fermentation. The opposite of anaerobic.

Agar   Similar to gelatine. A solidifying agent prepared from certain seaweeds. This, or gelatine, is sometimes used as a medium on which to grow yeast in a stoppered test tube. The tube is stored in a refrigerator and, when required, the stopper is taken off and a little of the yeast culture taken with an inoculating needle. It can be stored like this for nearly a year before the agar or gelatine dries.

Ageing   A process essential to every wine, although some wines need more than others. When new, a wine is usually harsh and requires time to mature into a smooth, fragrant liquid. While ageing, oxidation takes place, altering the characteristics of the wine and usually making it more mellow. The astringency of tannins is also smoothed and mellowed with age, and the more tannin in the wine the longer the ageing needs to be. Most flavours are lost with ageing; for instance, the addition of, say, cinnamon to an otherwise insipid white wine might give a pleasingly different flavour of cinnamon to the liquid. But over a period of time the flavour will change to the extent that, while perhaps still pleasant, it tastes nothing like cinnamon.

Air lock

Also called a fermentation trap. This is a device that excludes air from the fermentation, while allowing

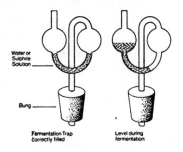

Water or Sulphite Solution

Bung

Fermentation Trap Correctly filled

Level during fermentation

the carbon dioxide given off to escape. This has the effect of excluding bacterial organisms and oxygen, upon which some bacteria thrive. The most popular is a glass U-tube with two bulbs. This is inserted through a bung and placed in the neck of the fermenting vessel. The U-bend of the lock is then filled with water sterilized by means of, for example, a Campden tablet. Thus the carbon dioxide bubbles out through the lock while air is excluded.

Albumen

Egg whites. In fresh or dried form they are often used as a fining agent for clearing wines. The whites are stirred into a portion of the wine and this is then mixed with the bulk and left to stand up to ten days before racking off. If too much albumen is used a protein haze will occur, so overfining should be avoided.

Alcohol

Pure spirit. One of the products of *Fermentation*. It is really the collective name of a group of alcohols, not all of which are found in wine. The principal alcohol produced in the process of wine fermentation is ethyl alcohol. (See also *Strength*.)

Aldehyde A fluid formed by the oxidation of alcohol. One of the organic chemical ingredients of wine. Aldehydes constitute a portion of the flavour of wine, particularly after ageing.

Almond The kernel of a stone-fruit from either of two trees (bitter almond and sweet almond). Although recipes for 'almond' wine are common, almond is never used on its own in a wine and is really a flavouring—one which has been popular for hundreds of years.

Amino acids Basic units of proteins. Fruits contain amino acids and these are thought to play an important part in the production of aroma and taste in wine.

Ammonium phosphate Phosphate is an essential requirement for fermentation. Where it is lacking, ammonium phosphate is often added.

Ammonium sulphate Yeast requires nitrogen for fermentation, and where this is lacking ammonium sulphate is often added as it is a rich source of nitrogen.

Anaerobic The stage of fermentation where air is excluded, usually by means of an air lock. The opposite of aerobic.

Apéritif An alcoholic liquid designed to be drunk before a meal as an appetizer.

Apple An excellent fruit for producing a white wine with good body. You will sometimes hear people complain that apple makes an insipid wine, but this is usually because the proportion of apples they are using is too low. Some recipes advocate as little as 4 lb of apples to the gallon of water, and this can indeed create an insipid wine. To give it good body, at least 10 lb of apples to the gallon is needed. While comparatively low in tannin and pectin, apples usually have adequate acid for wine production. Generally, crab- and cooking-apples make the best wine, and the worse the eating quality the better it is for wine.

Apple wine (*dry*)

Cooking apples	10–15 lb
Sugar	2½ lb
Tannin	½ teaspoon
Water	1 gallon

Yeast: Reisling
Nutrient

Crush or chop the apples, place in a container, bring the water to the boil and pour it over the apples. When cool, add the nutrient, tannin and yeast. Stir in 2½ lb of sugar to each gallon of liquid. Ferment aerobically for five days, then strain into fermentation jars and fit air locks.

Apricot　　Expensive to make from the fresh fruit, but a good white wine can be made from dried or tinned apricots. The fruit is rather high in pectin, so a depectinizer should always be used.

Apricot wine (*sweet*)

Dried apricots	1 lb
Sugar	3½ lb
Depectinizer	½ oz
Citric acid	teaspoon
Tannin	pinch

Yeast: Sauterne
Nutrient

Water	1 gallon

Method C. Aerobic fermentation two days.

Aroma　　In wine jargon aroma is different from bouquet. It is usually identified as being the smell of the fruit and constituents from which the wine is made. In fact some experts can differentiate not only the aroma of different fruits but also that of different varieties of grape! Aroma tends to diminish with ageing as bouquet develops.

Artichoke　　There are three distinct types of artichoke, the globe, Jerusalem and Chinese. The only variety I know that wine is made from is the tubers of the globe artichoke. I must admit I haven't got round to trying it yet, but I am informed that it makes an excellent dry wine. (For recipe, see Section Three.)

Asbestos pulp Used for clearing wine, but less frequently than it was, because it is inclined to taint the wine with an asbestos taste that takes a considerable time to wear off. It is also said that it removes some of the flavour of the wine.

Astringent Wine jargon referring to wines that make the mouth pucker, generally because of an excess of tannin. Most of the famous red wines are very astringent when young. With age, the tannin precipitates and the wine mellows.

Aubergine Purple fruit more commonly called egg-plant. It makes a reasonable dry white wine, but the aubergine must be ripe. If it isn't, it gives off a peculiar woody flavour that taints the wine. (Recipe, see Section Three.)

Autolysis If the wine is left on the yeast, or lees, for more than three months after fermentation has ceased, there is the possibility of the yeast decomposing—this is called autolysis.

B

Bacteria Kinds of microscopic unicellular organisms found everywhere. We are concerned here with the bacteria associated with wine. Bacteria are responsible for the malolactic fermentation, ropiness and acetification of wine, but, although wine will spoil if infected, the bacteria involved are not harmful to human beings, inasmuch as they do not transmit disease.

Balance Good balance is achieved when all the characteristics of a wine harmonize. Body, alcoholic content, astringency, acidity, flavour, sweetness and even colour must combine to produce a harmonic whole. For instance, a Sherry-type wine that is low in alcohol is unbalanced, as is a light white wine which is uncharacteristically heavy with tannin.

The one sure way to produce balanced wines is to keep accurate records, so that your mistakes are not repeated but your successes are.

Balm   A herb, the fresh leaves of which are often used in salads and summer drinks. The essential oil in the leaves and tender shoots impart a rather unusual aroma to wine made from balm leaves. Some people add raisins or sultanas to the recipe to give body, but this detracts from the flavour.

Balm wine (semi-sweet)

Balm leaves	2 quarts
Sugar	3½ lb
Citric acid	¾ oz
Tannin	pinch
Water	1 gallon

Yeast: Tokay
Nutrient

Method B. Aerobic fermentation five days.

Banana   Surprisingly, one of the most versatile fruits used in home winemaking. It is often used to add body to a wine weak in this respect; it also has a more neutral flavour than raisins. Both fresh or dry fruit can be used, but the dried variety sometimes gives rise to peculiar flavours. To give body to a wine of another fruit, 1 lb of bananas can be used to the gallon. Bananas are low in tannin, acid and pectin, but high in body and flavour.

Banana wine (semi-sweet)

Peeled bananas	4½ lb
Banana skins	½ lb
Sugar	3½ lb
Citric acid	¾ oz
Water	1 gallon

Yeast: Graves
Nutrient

Mash bananas and chop finely the skins; add sugar. Bring water to the boil and pour over fruit and sugar; stir. When cool, add acid, yeast and nutrient. Allow a two-day aerobic fermentation, strain well into fermenting vessel, fit air lock and ferment on.

Note: If you want a dry wine, reduce the sugar by 1 lb and add a pinch of tannin with the yeast and acid.

Barley
A cereal, barley is useful for making wine in the winter months when fresh fruit is not available. It makes an attractive dry white wine. Most wine-makers add raisins or other ingredients to the barley, but I find it has more character if used alone, and varied by use of different sugars and yeasts.

Barley wine (dry)

Barley	2 lb
Demerara sugar	$2\frac{1}{2}$ lb
Citric acid	$\frac{3}{4}$ oz
Tannin	pinch
Water	1 gallon
Yeast: Cereal	
Nutrient	

Soak the barley overnight in just enough water to cover it. Next morning put the barley through a mincer, add barley and sugar to the water and bring to the boil. When cool, add yeast, nutrient, acid and tannin. Allow a five-day aerobic fermentation, strain off into fermentation jar, fit air lock and ferment on. If a richer wine is required, increase sugar to $3\frac{1}{2}$ lb and omit tannin.

Barrel
In wine terms, a container, usually wood and preferably oak, in which wine is stored, aged and sometimes shipped. Generally a cask is identical, but larger; as a rough guide, a barrel of wine is movable, a cask is not. Barrels are frequently used by the home winemaker because of their larger storage capacity and the fact that wine matures better in a wooden

barrel. When new, an oak barrel will infuse additional tannin into the wine and make it very astringent, requiring extensive ageing to mellow.

New barrels should be filled to the brim with fresh water and left for five days. After being emptied, it is refilled with a solution of 4 oz of soda in each gallon of boiling water and left for two days. Empty again and rinse with a solution of four Campden tablets and $\frac{1}{4}$ oz of citric acid to each gallon of water. Empty and rinse with fresh water.

Second-hand barrels must be sterilized (never buy one that smells of vinegar). Fill with a solution of 2 oz of domestic bleach to every 5 gallons of water for twenty-four hours. Empty, rinse with fresh water, fill with fresh water and leave for two days, empty, fill again with fresh water and leave another two days.

An important point is always to keep the barrel on a stand, never on the ground on its side where the centre stave takes all the weight.

Always keep barrels full and topped up, otherwise the wine will spoil. Even when not in use, keep the barrel full of clear, sulphited water. If the barrel is allowed to dry the wood will shrink and the barrel may be ruined.

Plastic barrels are available, but it is doubtful whether wine will mature in them as well as it does in wood.

Beaujolais One of the best-known French wines, mostly red, made from the gamay grape. When the home winemaker tries to produce a commercial red-type wine he often ends up with a Beaujolais-style wine when successful. A recipe for making a wine similar to Beaujolais is given in Section Three.

Beaumé A scale used on hydrometers designed for testing the sugar content of a must by measuring its density.

Bees wine This is not really a wine but a description of the action of a certain type of yeast—Saccharomyces priformis. This particular yeast forms clumps, and the escaping carbon dioxide in the fermenting must carries the clumps to the surface, whereupon they promptly sink down again. The consequent up-and-down action has been likened to a busy hive of bees, hence the name.

Beet sugar If you can obtain sugar beet it makes an excellent dry white wine. It is easily fermentable and, being relatively low in flavour, blends well with other ingredients.

Beet Sugar wine (dry)

Sugar beet	4 lb
Sugar	2 lb 4 oz
Citric acid	teaspoon
Tannin	pinch
Water	1 gallon
Yeast: All Purpose	
Nutrient	

Chop the beet finely. Place in water and boil for one hour, adding the sugar just before removing from heat. When cool, add yeast, nutrient, acid and tannin and stir well. Strain into fermentation jar, fit air lock and ferment on.

Beetroot A vegetable, but none the less popular with home winemakers. It makes a beautifully coloured red wine, but during fermenting, and in bottle, it must be kept away from light, otherwise the bright red turns to a dull brown. It is best to buy the beetroot uncooked. Just scrub it and leave the skin on.

Beetroot wine (semi-sweet)

Beetroot	6 lb
Brown sugar	3 lb
Citric acid	$\frac{1}{4}$ oz
Water	1 gallon
Yeast: Port	
Nutrient	

Chop beetroot into small pieces. Cook gently in the water until tender, adding the sugar just before removing from the heat. When cool add yeast, acid and nutrient. Stir, strain into fermenting jar, fit air lock and ferment on.

Bentonite A montmorillonite clay used for clarifying wine. Its action is often quite miraculous, used properly, but it does have its disadvantages. If too much is used it gives the wine a disagreeable earthy flavour, so a small trial batch should be attempted before treating a large amount of wine. It keeps indefinitely, but must be prepared at least twenty-four hours before using. Nevertheless it is probably one of the best clarifying agents and should be considered if straining through a bag fails.

Bilberry The blue-black berries of the bilberry are deservedly one of the most popular fruits in home winemaking. It is, admittedly, a fiddly job collecting the fresh fruit, but excellent wine can be made from dried bilberries. The fruit is high in tannin and flavour and adequate in respect of body, acid and sugar, but as only something like 3 lb are used in a gallon of water, most of these ingredients have to be added. It most suitably makes a Burgundy- or Port-type wine. If using the dried fruit, smell the berries closely and if they smell musty at all reject them.

Bilberry wine (dry)

Fresh bilberries	4 lb
or	
Dried bilberries	$\frac{3}{4}$ lb
Sugar	$2\frac{3}{4}$ lb
Citric acid	$\frac{3}{4}$ oz
Water	1 gallon
Yeast: Burgundy	
Nutrient	

Method B. Aerobic fermentation five days.

It is very economical to do a second run on the remainder of the bilberry pulp after straining. Just place the remains in a container and repeat the procedure exactly, adding sugar, acid, yeast and nutrient. You will get a lighter-coloured wine, not so rich in tannin, which you may prefer. Some people even do a third run, which results in a rose-style wine.

Binning
When bottled wine is laid away for ageing or storing, it is said to be 'binned', and the larger cellars frequently have areas numbered so that a bottle may have no more than, say, 'bin 14' marked on it, to be labelled at a more suitable time. (See *Storing*.)

Birch sap
Sap from the birch tree makes an excellent wine. It was once a very popular drink in Russia. However, it must be noted that, while a mature tree will suffer little if a gallon of sap is taken while the sap is rising, every two years or so, the tree will die if you get too enthusiastic. Make sure that the tree is mature—at least 10 inches in circumference; and that the sap is rising—generally around the first fortnight in March.

A hole just wide enough to take a bored rubber bung should be drilled, upwards at 45 degrees. Place a length of tubing in the bung and insert the bung in the hole. Lead the tubing into a gallon fermenting jar filling the remaining space in the neck of the jar with cottonwool to prevent insects and foreign matter contaminating the sap. When the jar is nearly full, remove the bung and plug the hole in the tree tightly with a cork bung; if you don't the tree may die. It should take about two days to fill the jar, but in any case the draining should not be carried on longer than three days.

Birch sap wine (dry)

Birch sap	1 gallon
Sugar	2½ lb
Citric acid	½ oz

Tannin   pinch
Yeast: Reisling or Graves
Nutrient

Bring the sap to the boil. This is merely to sterilize it, and some people say that this destroys the delicate flavour. As an alternative, dissolve two Campden tablets in the sap and leave for twenty-four hours. When cool, or after twenty-four hours, stir in the sugar, acid, yeast, tannin and nutrient. Pour into fermentation jar, fit air lock and ferment on. Some people add raisins and/or orange peel while boiling and strain off before fermenting, but you should really taste the wine from sap alone first, as any addition completely destroys the character. If a sweeter wine is desired increase the sugar by $\frac{3}{4}$ lb and omit tannin.

Bitterness   Usually perceptible in the aftertaste of a wine. This is more often a fault in grape wines when there has been a very dry year, but little is known about the actual cause. The main culprits would seem to be unsuitable yeast and/or a lack of acidity during fermentation. There is only one cure—ageing—but this is not 100 per cent certain to work.

Blackberry   Known also as bramble, the blackberry is obviously a very economical fruit if one has access to nearby hedgerows. It makes an excellent red wine, although the colour tends to deteriorate, especially if kept in the light. High in acid, but adequate in all other respects, it is a useful fruit for a wide range of wine styles.

Blackberry wine (*semi-sweet*)

Blackberries   6 lb
Sugar $3\frac{1}{2}$ lb
Yeast: Burgundy
Nutrient

Method B. Aerobic fermentation four days.

Black currant	See *Currants*.
Blending	This refers to the practice of mixing wines of different characteristics, flavour or age, and is carried out for varying reasons. Blending can be undertaken to produce wine of a uniform nature every year—a task beyond the scope of the average home winemaker —or to produce a palatable wine from a variety of wines that are less palatable. For instance, if you have a wine that is too acid, and another that is too sweet, a little experiment in blending a small portion might well result in something that pleases you. In any event it is wise to err on the side of caution, because blending is a skill that takes quite a while to acquire.
Blueberry	A shrub, and a native of North America, the fruit of the blueberry makes good wine and should be treated the same as bilberry.
Blue fining	A complex process of fining that must be carried out by a skilled chemist. As such it is of little interest to the home winemaker.
Body	A full-bodied wine is often considered as being high in alcohol—but this is incorrect usage. A wine that is lacking in body is thin and watery. Full body is not always a desired characteristic; a delicate Gooseberry or Apple wine made with little fruit would be unbalanced if it had body, while a deep red Bilberry or Elderberry would be lacking without it.
Boiling	Effective as a method of sterilization provided a temperature of at least 185°F (85°C) is reached. And it must be remembered that if solids such as apple or parsnip are present in the liquid, it will be necessary to maintain the temperature for a minute or two so that the centre of the solids reach the required temperature.
	The use of boiling water to sterilize glass and metal must be considered inferior to using a good sterilizing solution. Apart from the dangers involved in manipulating large containers of boiling water,

glassware needs to be handled very carefully, and even then there is a high risk of breakage.

If a wine is boiled either to sterilize, rehydrate dried fruit or extract sugar, it must be noted that boiling can destroy the more delicate flavour such as elderflower, and if continued can result in a 'cooked' taste in the wine. Also, some fruits—figs are an example—if boiled will produce a cloudy wine that is virtually impossible to clear.

Borax Glycerine of borax can be used in the U-bend of an air lock. It has the advantage over a sulphite solution in that it will not deteriorate.

Bordeaux See *Claret*.

Borer A tool for boring holes in corks so that air locks can be fitted.

Bottle The final repository of the wine (if we omit the glass and the stomach!). Generally red wines reside in bottles of green glass and white wines in clear glass, although that is not always the case. If you intend to submit your wine in a home winemaking contest, whatever the wine it must be presented in a bottle of clear glass.

All wines age more quickly in small bottles, and the larger the bottle the longer the maturation process takes.

There is a great variety of wine-bottle shapes, but it is a mistake to think that a specific shape belongs to only one type of wine—the Bordeaux straight-sided bottle, for instance, is used in virtually every country in the world.

Sometimes bottles are marked. When a fortified wine such as Port is bottled, after a while it forms a heavy sediment or crust along the lowermost side of the bottle. So that this crust is not disturbed a white patch is painted on the uppermost neck of the bottle so that the bottle is never turned round and the crust broken.

When storing empty bottles, make sure they are washed out in hot soapy water and rinsed in a sulphite solution before storing. Old wine will line the sides or bottom of a bottle and it is a very hard job to clean off once it has dried. Try to store empty bottles upside down so that they won't be full of dust when you require them. And talking of cleaning bottles, there is a bottle-cleaning brush that has a bend in it that is a worthwhile utensil to possess.

Bouquet Not to be confused with aroma. Bouquet is the combination of intriguing, pleasant and good odours given off by a well-made mature wine, and comes mainly from esters developed by slow oxidation of elements in the wine.

Bramble The popular name in the north of England for the blackberry.

Brass Utensils of brass can be affected by acid in the wine and this can cause cloudiness and bad flavour. It is a metal to be avoided in winemaking.

Brilliant This is the word for a wine that is absolutely clear, with no trace of sediment or cloudiness even when held up to a strong light in a clear bottle.

Broad bean Possibly the hardiest of vegetables, the broad bean can be made into an adequate wine of the dry variety. It can also be made sweet, but this adds a flavour which some find disagreeable. The liquor made from boiling can also be incorporated with other ingredients, but try it on its own first.

Broad bean wine (dry)

Shelled broad beans	4 lb
Sugar	$2\frac{1}{2}$ lb
Citric acid	$\frac{1}{4}$ oz
Tannin	pinch
Water	1 gallon
Yeast: All Purpose	
Nutrient	

Place the beans in the water and bring to the boil. Try not to touch the beans because, if the skins break, the wine will be cloudy. Turn the heat off as soon as the water boils. Carefully strain off the liquor and add sugar. When cool add acid, tannin, yeast and nutrient, pour into fermentation jar, fit air lock and ferment on.

This is the basic recipe, although I prefer about ¼ lb of minced sultanas added to the beans before boiling.

Broom
A beautiful flowering shrub, the flowers of which make a good, delicate wine. Also known as Cytisus.

Broom wine (sweet)

Broom flowers	1 gallon
Sugar	3½ lb
Citric acid	½ oz
Campden tablet	1
Water	1 gallon
Yeast: Sauterne	
Nutrient	

Method A. Aerobic fermentation five days.

Buchner flask
A vessel used for filtering wine through a very fine paper filter by means of a suction pump.

Bucket
A winemaker will often work with absolutely sterile equipment while using a dirty old bucket for transferring liquid. A bucket should be kept scrupulously clean, inside and outside; when rinsing with sterilizing fluid don't forget the outside of the rim with which liquid is in slight contact as you pour. Make sure the bucket is not of an unsuitable metal and, if you carry out aerobic fermentation in a plastic bucket, make sure that it is a high-density plastic—some of the cheap plastics taint the wine.

Bullace
Tiny plums, smaller than damsons, frequently called wild plums. (For recipe, see under *Plum*; goes best with a Burgundy yeast.)

Bung
A sealer or stopper used for sealing an opening in a cask, container or fermentation jar. When drilled through the middle a bung will take an air lock. The usual materials are cork or rubber. Cork has to be sterilized properly and, when drilled or bored, may

not always be absolutely airtight—an essential requirement. For this reason, and the ease of sterilizing, rubber bungs are becoming more popular. Rubber fills in all the crevices and makes an absolutely airtight seal.

Burdock Although similar in appearance, the burdock is not related to the dock family. A wild plant, the foliage is used to make wine and the root for beer.

Burdock wine (sweet)

Burdock leaves and burrs	$\frac{1}{2}$ lb
Brown sugar	4 lb
Citric acid	$\frac{1}{2}$ oz
Campden tablet	1
Water	1 gallon
Yeast: Tokay	
Nutrient	

Method A. Aerobic fermentation five days.

Burgundy This area, south-east of Paris, is famous for red, white and sometimes rosé wines; but here we apply the name only to the red, which is a luscious dry wine somewhat sweeter in character than claret. (Recipe for making a Burgundy-type wine is given in Section Three.)

Burnet The Greater Salad Burnet is a perennial herb with stems up to 2 feet high, the dark crimson or purple flowers of which make an attractive rosé-style wine.

Burnet wine (dry)

Burnet flowers	1 gallon
Sugar	$2\frac{1}{2}$ lb
Campden tablet	1
Citric acid	$\frac{1}{2}$ oz
Water	1 gallon
Tannin	pinch
Yeast: Chablis	
Nutrient	

Method A. Aerobic fermentation three days.

C

Cabbage   A vegetable that needs no introduction as an edible item, but some may be surprised to hear that wine can be made from it. However, I must confess that I find it difficult to make even a tolerable wine from cabbage alone. Perhaps it is my fault, but just in case I have selected a recipe which includes raisins.

Cabbage wine (semi-sweet)

Cabbage, shredded	3 lb
Raisins, minced	½ lb
Sugar	3 lb
Citric acid	½ oz
Tannin	pinch
Water	1 gallon
Yeast: All Purpose Nutrient	

Method B. Aerobic fermentation five days.

Campden tablets   A proprietary preparation used in sterilization of utensils, bottles and wine. It consists of potassium metabisulphite and is very convenient to use. Two tablets dissolved in a pint of water (or pro rata) is a useful solution for rinsing bottles and utensils, while one tablet per gallon of must will help keep down undesirable organisms. Further, an additional tablet per gallon in the finished wine will help eliminate fermentation in bottle. Campden does taste in wine, but the taste wears off with ageing. If used in the must, at least twenty-four hours should elapse before the yeast is introduced.

Cane sugar   Makes a useful wine; use in the same way as *Beet sugar*.

Canned food   Deserving of a book on the subject—and one exists. I can do no better than refer you to the bibliography at the back of this book which lists 'Winemaking with Canned and Dried Fruit'.

Most tinned fruits can be made into excellent wine, but there are two dangers. Ensure that the label indicates that the contents consist solely of fruit and sugar, because if there are preservatives present the must might not ferment; also, if a sweetener other than sugar is included it might not be converted during fermentation—and you will get a sweet wine whether you like it or not.

Cap
When solids are introduced into the wine must they invariably sink to the bottom. But when the yeast starts fermenting the solids rise to the surface, forming a dense mass known as the cap.

Capsule
Used to cover the neck and cork and, while designed mainly to protect the cork from bacterial attack, serves the additional function in that it makes the bottle more attractive. Lead was extensively used, but less so now, the most popular being the crimped alloy variety which can be easily fitted by hand. There is also a shrink-fitting plastic capsule which is becoming more popular.

Caramel
Burnt sugar, used in the kitchen as a flavouring medium. It is sometimes used by the home winemaker to impart a Sherry flavour to a wine.

Caramelized
The condition of a wine that has spent too much time near a source of heat and consequently develops a caramel taint.

Caraway
Caraway seeds are sometimes used as an addition in flower wines, in which case up to 1 oz of caraway can be added to the flower heads.

Carbohydrates
A group which includes starch, sugar, gum and pectin, some or all of which are found in winemaking ingredients.

Carbon
Better known in the form of charcoal, carbon can be used to reduce colour and remove bad taste in a wine. But it is important to know what grade of carbon, to use; careful tests must be made beforehand to establish the correct dose. It is of little value to the winemaker who lacks laboratory facilities and training.

Carbon dioxide	A colourless, odourless gas that is given off during the process of fermentation.
Carboy	A large globular glass bottle that will hold several gallons of liquid. It is usually protected in a metal frame and is often used for the carriage of certain acids. Despite its relative fragility, it is excellent for storing wine in.
Carnation	More often found in a buttonhole, carnation heads can be used to produce wine. The recipe is identical to that listed under *Broom wine*, except that in the case of carnation the amount of flower heads must be halved.
Carrot	Possibly one of the best vegetables from which wine is made. A well-made Carrot wine is very rich in flavour and is good for both sweet and dry styles.

Carrot wine (dry)

Carrots	6 lb
Sugar	2½ lb
Citric acid	½ oz
Tannin	pinch
Water	1 gallon
Yeast: Reisling	
Nutrient	

Scrub carrots but do not peel; put through a mincer. Place carrots in water and bring to the boil, stirring in sugar. Simmer for fifteen minutes. When cool, strain into fermentation jar, add acid, tannin, yeast and nutrient. Plug neck of fermentation jar with cottonwool until fermentation commences, then fit air lock and ferment on.

Casein	A material containing amino acid that is one of the principal constituents of cheese and milk. It has the unique advantage in that it can be used as a fining or decolouring agent without affecting the flavour, but it must be used under the most stringent conditions. Because of this it is not recommended for the amateur.

Cask   See *Barrel*.

Celery   Not the most popular of vegetables for making wine, but some people swear by it and produce excellent wine to back up their claims. Others find it insipid. The following is worth a try.

Celery wine (sweet)

Celery	6 lb
Sugar	3½ lb
Citric acid	½ oz
Water	1 gallon
Yeast: All Purpose	
Nutrient	

Use only all-white celery; the green variety which is becoming more popular is not so suitable for wine.

Clean the celery and chop finely. Cover with the water and bring to the boil; simmer until tender and add the sugar while stirring. When cool, add acid, yeast and nutrient, strain into fermentation jar. Plug neck of jar with cottonwool until fermentation commences, then fit air lock and ferment on.

Cellar   Technically, a storage space for wine. This could be at the top of a skyscraper, but traditionally it is usually underground for the simple reason that the correct temperatures are easier to maintain. The important thing is that the wine cellar should be located where the most suitable conditions exist— not just where there is space.

A good cellar should be dark, free from vibration and with sufficient ventilation to ensure that it is not too damp. The temperature should be consistently even throughout the year, an ideal temperature being around 55°F (12°C), although a minimum of 45°F (8°C) or a maximum of 65°F (18°C) could be tolerated. The important thing is that the temperature should be constant.

With modern living it is becoming more difficult to find suitable cellar space for your wine, but unless you produce for almost immediate consumption it pays to ensure that your wines are suitably stored. It is pointless going to great pains to produce good-quality wine if it is ruined by storing in, say, an attic.

Cellulose pulp   Sometimes used as a filter medium as an alternative to a filter paper. It is moistened and inserted into a filter, ensuring that excess moisture is sucked in before the wine is poured through. In fact it is best to pour boiling water through the pulp several times before treating the wine, otherwise a peculiar paper-like aftertaste can occur in the wine.

Centaury   Or Knapweed, a plant of the genus Cornflower. It imparts a rather bitter taste to liquids and because of this is sometimes used to produce a bitter, or bitter-sweet apéritif-style wine. Use no more than ½ lb of the fresh plant, or one-quarter of this amount of the dried, which can be obtained from health stores, to the gallon of finished wine.

Cereal   This includes rice, barley, wheat and dried maize, all of which can be converted into good wine when other ingredients are unavailable. In previous years the problem of cereal wine has been the occurrence of starch hazes, but this can be minimized now by using a cereal yeast. (See under respective headings.)

Chablis   An area south-east of Paris which produces some of the most famous white Burgundies. Chablis is one of the best wines to drink with fish—especially shellfish. (A recipe for making a Chablis-type wine is given in Section Three.)

Chalk   Precipitated chalk is sometimes added at the rate of ½ oz to the gallon to correct for over-acidity. If this is done, add the chalk before fermentation. Added at a later date it often leaves a taste.

Chamomile   The flower heads are used. Chamomile has a very powerful, fragrant scent which, while producing an excellent wine, can be disastrous if too much is used. Use the recipe for *Broom wine*, cutting down the flower heads to only one-quarter of the amount.

Champagne   A bubbling, effervescent drink, Champagne is the king of white wines and certainly the most popular for parties and celebrations. Because of this—and the price—many home winemakers try their hand at Champagne-type wines, and with a great deal of success. However, the process of fermentation may produce great pressure within the bottle, and an exploding bottle can be fatal. (See also p. 124.)

Chaptalization   In the wine trade, this is the term used when a grower adds sugar to the grapes to turn what would have been a thin, acid wine into an acceptable one. This can happen when the weather has been poor. Countries vary as to the amount—if any—that it can be practised.

Charcoal   See *Carbon.*

Charlock   Or Wild Mustard. A nuisance to farmers, it makes an excellent wine. Both flowers and leaves are used and the recipe for *Broom wine* can be followed.

Cherry   There are many varieties of cherry, all of which make good wine, the morello being the best. As with all stone-fruits, cherries are high in pectin and so it is essential that a depectinizer is used.

Cherry wine (sweet)

Eating-cherries (weighed whole, then stoned)	8 lb
Sugar	$3\frac{1}{2}$ lb
Citric acid	$\frac{1}{2}$ oz
Depectinizer	$\frac{1}{2}$ oz
Water	1 gallon
Yeast: Port	
Nutrient	

Method B. Aerobic fermentation five days.

For a dry wine use morello cherries, omit citric acid and reduce sugar to $2\frac{1}{2}$ lb. Add one crushed Campden tablet with the depectinizer, and a pinch of tannin.

Chervil	An annual herb, the fresh leaves of which are used to impart an aniseed flavour to salads, sauces and soups. In winemaking the root or plant is used to give flavour in conjunction with other ingredients, particularly rhubarb or parsnip. In this case up to 2 lb of root or 2 pints of leaves and/or flower heads can be added to the must.
Chianti	One of the best-known Italian wines often seen in the popular wicker flasks, although the best Chianti comes in straight-sided bottles. It is made from the Trebbiano, San Gioveto and Cannaiolo grapes. True Chianti is now only red, although previously there was a white variety. (A recipe for making Chianti-type wine is given in Section Three.)
Cider	Not a wine, but a very refreshing drink of low or medium alcohol content. It is made basically from the juice of apples, fermented without added sugar. If a sweet cider is desired, sweeten with saccharin to taste. A pinch of tannin or citric acid may be added to improve the taste.
Citral	Some plants contain essential oils which impart distinctive flavours to finished wine. Lemon oil, for instance, is rich in the terpene citral.
Citrus	A genus or group which includes lime, grapefruit, orange, lemon, etc.
Cladosporium cellare	A mould frequently seen growing in commercial cellars. It is often encouraged because it is said to be able to absorb bad smells and keep the cellar sweet.
Claret	The traditional name for the red wines of Bordeaux. Red Bordeaux is famed as the finest red wine in the world, and the very best command top prices. It is slightly more astringent than Burgundy when young, but in maturity is preferred by the majority of wine experts. (A recipe for a Claret-type wine is given in Section Three.)
Clarifying	Rendering a hazy wine brilliant by means of fining or filtering. A wine will usually clarify naturally if given time.

Clarity	Means the same thing as *Brilliance*.
Clary	A popular wine in some parts. It is made from the blue flowers of Clary Sage. Use the recipe for *Broom wine*, but reduce the amount of blossom by half.
Clearing	Another word for *Clarifying*.
Clinitest	A preparation sold in chemists. Used mainly by diabetics for checking the sugar content of liquids. It can be used for determining the residual sugar content of wine. (See *Residual sugar*.)
Cloths	Various types can be used for filtering or straining wine. A cloth should be well washed and thoroughly rinsed in fresh water—then taste it! It is surprising how a cloth can impart a taint to wine. Ensure that no particles of fluff are still working loose, because you don't want to add this to your fermenting must.
Clove	A popular culinary item, clove is usually used as an additional flavouring. However, Clove wine is enjoyed by some, particularly warmed on a cold winter's night, or as a base for home-made liqueurs.

Clove wine (sweet)

Cloves	1 oz
Brown sugar	$3\frac{1}{2}$ lb
Citric acid	$\frac{1}{2}$ oz
Water	1 gallon
Yeast: All Purpose	
Nutrient	

Well bruise the cloves, add to the water with the sugar, bring to the boil and simmer for ten minutes. When cool, strain into fermentation jar, add acid, yeast and nutrient. Plug neck of jar with cottonwool until fermentation commences, then fit air lock and ferment on.

Clover	The enemy of the gardener, clover blossom is popular as a wine. Use the recipe for *Broom wine*, reducing the quantity of blossom to three-quarters.
Coffee	More popular as a beverage, coffee makes a novel

wine, particularly when made sweet, although some prefer it dry.

Coffee wine (*sweet*)

Coffee	$\frac{1}{2}$ lb
Brown sugar	$3\frac{1}{2}$ lb
Citric acid	$\frac{1}{2}$ oz
Water	1 gallon

Yeast: Sauterne
Nutrient

Pour the coffee and sugar into the water and bring to the boil. Leave to cool, then strain into fermentation jar and add acid, yeast and nutrient. Plug neck of jar with cottonwool until fermentation commences, then fit air lock and ferment on. For a dry wine reduce sugar to $2\frac{1}{2}$ lb and add a pinch of tannin with the acid.

Colt's-foot   A wild perennial flower abundant in Britain. The flower itself makes a wine that is very popular in some parts. Use the recipe for *Broom wine*.

Competitions   There is not space here to go into all the aspects of wine competitions. Suffice to say that most wine circles hold them and there are also competitions of a national nature. Try to enter both types regularly; you will improve your wine, increase your interest and, most important, enjoy your wine more. (See *Exhibiting*.)

Concentrates   This refers to concentrated juices, or pulp, and is becoming more popular each year. Grape concentrate, for instance, does not entail messy pulping and an always potentially dangerous aerobic fermentation. There is a variety of concentrates now available in various types of fruit—try your hand at some, you will be pleasantly surprised. It is impossible to go into details of recipes here, as concentrates vary in their degrees of concentration, but if you buy some from a home winemaking shop or department there will be the recommended recipe on the tin or jar.

Containers   We are not talking about barrels or casks here, but containers such as pails that wine is in for a short time. Glass is best, but fragile. Pottery is fine, but beware some older varieties with a lead glaze. Plastic should be of a hard density material: the softer, cheaper types often taint the wine. In any case, it is best not to leave wine in plastic containers for too long.

Copper   This metal is somewhat soluble in solutions of fruit acids and will give rise to bad-tasting wine. Avoid it at all costs.

Corking tools   The most simple tool for this job is a 'flogger', which is actually just a piece of heavy wood with a flat top which is used to bang or 'flog' corks home with. It is a most exasperating instrument!

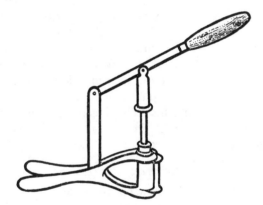

On the other hand, there are tools on the market which will suitably compress a cork and drive it home in one simple movement. These are simple to use, and with one you can cork hundreds of bottles without much bother.

Corks   The 'stopper'-type corks with either cork or wooden caps or tops are very popular—in fact, essential for competitions—but are not very suitable if you are storing a wine for any length of time.

The straight-sided cork is deservedly the most used.

It should be light in colour and with few blemishes. If possible obtain extra-long corks for wines such as Elderberry which need long ageing, because the longer you intend to keep the wine the longer the cork should be.

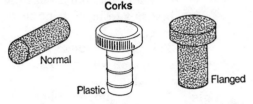

Corks

Plastic corks are creeping into favour but would be even more used if all bottles had exactly the same diameter at the pouring end. Unfortunately they vary fractionally and you will find that your plastic cork is almost impossible to insert into one make of bottle, yet almost drops into another, making a dubious seal. The main advantage of plastic 'corks' is that they are easier to sterilize if re-used. And (no one ever mentions this) if they are a good fit they enable the wine to be stored in upright bottles!

Cornmeal wine (Golden Dinamite) This recipe has been formulated by Messrs Hidalgo, who import grape juice concentrates and is well worth a try.

Cornmeal wine (medium)

Yellow cornmeal or cornflower	2 lb
Sugar	3 lb
Lemons (juice)	2
Oranges (juice)	3
Grape juice concentrate	3 pints
Tartaric acid	1 oz
Ammonium phosphate	$\frac{1}{4}$ oz
Ground rice	$\frac{1}{4}$ oz
Campden tablets	2
Water	2 gallons
Yeast	

Country wine   Usually defined as a wine derived from basic ingre-
                     dients that are available locally—usually free—such
                     as wild fruits or flowers and baker's yeast saved from
                     the last batch of bread.

Cowslip   Cowslip is a wild flower. Use the recipe for *Broom
                     wine* and the same method (A).

Crab apple   The original apple. It is from the crab that all
                     orchard apples evolved. Sour and small, it never-
                     theless makes better Apple wine than dessert apples.

Cranberry   A fruit almost identical to the bilberry in physical
                     characteristics. For wine use the same recipe and
                     method as for *Bilberry*.

Cream of   See *Acid, Tartaric*.
Tartar

Cultures of   A yeast produced under laboratory conditions as
yeast   opposed to the indigenous wild yeast present on the
                     skins of fruit, vegetables and practically everything
                     else.

Cup   A drink made up from finished products. It can
                     contain wine, beer, cider and/or a small measure of
                     spirits and sweetened with sugar, treacle or honey,
                     depending on the recipe. Local areas have their own
                     traditional 'cups', or you can invent your own.

Currant   Whether black, red or white, currants make an
                     excellent wine, although the flavour is a little too
                     strong for some people; in which case you can use
                     slightly less currants, but then you do lose some
                     body.

Black, White or Red Currant wine (sweet)

Crushed fresh currants	3 lb
Sugar	$3\frac{1}{2}$ lb
Depectinizer	$\frac{1}{2}$ oz
Citric acid	$\frac{1}{4}$ oz
Water	1 gallon
Yeast: According to currant	
Nutrient	

Method C. Aerobic fermentation five days.

Cyser   Some people insist that pure apple juice and honey
                 be used; others that 1–2 lb of apples to the gallon
                 of water is sufficient. It is really only Apple wine
                 using honey instead of sugar. The cyser is named
                 according to the apple variety, i.e. Russet Cyser,
                 Laxton Cyser, etc.

                                    D

Damson   A fruit of the plum family. It contains a high
                 percentage of pectin and must be treated accord-
                 ingly. It makes a good red wine which, in my
                 opinion, is slightly inferior to Plum.

                 Damson wine (medium)

Stoned damsons	6 lb
Sugar	3 lb
Depectinizer	$\frac{3}{4}$ oz
Water	1 gallon

                 Yeast: Port or Tokay
                 Nutrient

                 Method B. Aerobic fermentation four days.

Dandelion   A weed or a delicious green salad according to your
                 taste, the dandelion was at one time famous in
                 combination—Dandelion and Burdock is still made
                 though now less popular. The wine is made from
                 the dandelion flower.

                 Dandelion wine (dry)

Dandelion flowers	2 quarts
Sugar	$2\frac{1}{2}$ lb
Oranges (juice)	4
Water	1 gallon

                 Yeast: Chablis
                 Nutrient

                 Method B. Aerobic fermentation not less than one
                 day but definitely no more than two days.

Darkening   Occurs in white wine—or rather it is more noticeable than in red. Leave a glass of white wine out for a few days and if it goes dark it is not stable and the addition of a stabilizer such as Campden tablets or a proprietary preparation is required. Of course an unstable wine takes a long time to darken in bottle, but this does occur and is caused by oxidation.

Date   A dried fruit which deserves to be used more frequently; on its own it provides both flavour and body and can with benefit be used in combination with other fruits.

Date wine (dry)

Chopped stoned dates	4 lb
Demerara sugar	½ lb
Citric acid	½ oz
Tannin	pinch
Water	1 gallon
Yeast: All Purpose	
Nutrient	

Method B. Aerobic fermentation five days.

Decanting   The act of transferring a wine from its original bottle to another vessel, usually prior to serving. It is done for one of two reasons: to separate the wine from its sediment; or to present it in a more attractive or clearer vessel.

Demerara   A dark brown sugar that deepens the colour of a wine, so don't use it if you want your white wine to be a delicate straw colour. It also has a pronounced taste so should not be used in recipes which use delicate flower heads and the like. It can favourably be used in Port- or Sherry-type wines or to add a little interest to an otherwise uninteresting recipe.

Depectinizer   See *Pectolase*.

Dessert wine   A wine that would most properly be served with dessert, whatever its alcoholic strength, such as Sauterne, Port, sweet Sherry, etc.

Dewberry	A hybrid relative of the blackberry. Treat it the same, using the same recipe.
Diabetic wine	There is of course no such thing but the term is used of a wine that has completely fermented all the available sugar. To ensure a sugar-free wine never use more than $2\frac{1}{2}$ lb of sugar to each gallon of water —and less sugar if the main ingredient contains natural sugar such as date or raisin. And always use ample yeast nutrient to ensure thorough fermentation.
Diluting	Dilution (with water) can be carried out for several reasons—to reduce the gravity of a liquid, for instance. Some juices such as grapefruit are too acid in the neat state and so have to be diluted. Then again, some fruit juices such as black currant are very high in flavour so the fruit or juice is diluted.
Diseases of wine	Disease in any language is a nasty word, and wine has as many problems as anything in this direction. Diseases or faults in wine range from turning it to vinegar via the bacteria acetobacter; autolysis; hazes; acidity, etc. They are all dealt with under their respective titles.
Disgorging	Champagne and similar wines undergo a second fermentation in the bottle. During this process the corked bottles are slanted downwards so that the yeast forms at the neck. When ready the cork is swiftly removed and replaced while the bottle is still pointing downwards (it takes practice, believe me!) and the resulting portion of liquid that escapes takes the yeast sediment with it. The technique is called disgorging.
Drake tube	A tall tube containing a hydrometer for taking the specific gravity of wine or beer.
Dry	In wine language, the opposite to sweet. A wine is said to be dry when all trace of sugar has been fermented out.

E

Egg shell
This is often used to clear and/or decolour a white wine. Clean the shell and bake it gently in the oven and then crush it into powder. When added to the wine the particles will continually rise and sink. When they finally settle down the wine should be clear. A fairly thick sediment will probably occur, so rack the wine off well clear of this.

Egg white
A good fining for both red and white wine. It has the disadvantage that it is easy to overfine—in other words, if you put too much in, the wine will never clear. As the ratio is approximately three-quarters of an egg white (thoroughly mixed into a pint or so of the wine and then added back to the bulk) to 10 gallons of wine you can see that you have to make your wine in large quantities or be very careful.

Elderberry
An excellent fruit for home winemaking, it has been called the 'English grape' due to its popularity. It is virtually identical in physical characteristics to Bilberry but has a higher tannin content and therefore needs to be (*a*) kept in the bottle for at least two years or (*b*) fermented on the pulp for no more than two days. The trouble is the latter course robs the elderberry of some of its best characteristics. Use the recipe as for *Bilberry*, but use a Bordeaux yeast.

Enzymes
A book could be written about enzymes alone. They play an essential part in the process of fermentation, in fact it is the enzymes which are responsible for the alcoholic fermentation of sugar. It is enzymes which produce heat in the fermentation, and they are precipitated by alcohol; this is why the fermentation slows down as the alcoholic content gets higher.

The home winemaker will probably be more familiar with the depectinizing enzyme which breaks down the pectin structures that would otherwise cloud a wine.

Esters
With age, the alcohol and acids in a wine combine to form esters. It is a widely held opinion that esters

form part of the aroma of an ageing wine, but modern findings suggest that they have little or no aroma.

Estufa
Or Estufagem: the process used in making Madeira wine. In more ancient and leisurely days wine was often stowed in the hold of a ship travelling to the East Indies. The journey in the hot, stifling hold imparted a curious flavour that pleased some people and also increased the life of the wine in bottle. The Estufagem was designed to simulate the effects of such a voyage by holding the wine at a certain temperature for a specified time. (For details of the process, see Section Three under *Madeira*.)

Ethyl acetate
One of the esters—but not a very nice one. Ethyl alcohol can combine with acetic acid to produce ethyl acetate, and any more than a fraction of pure ethyl acetate will spoil the wine. But this shouldn't bother you if you make sure that no acetic acid is in your wine in the first place!

Ethyl alcohol
The principal alcohol produced in the fermentation of wine.

Evaporation
This means exactly the same as the definition in your dictionary, and in wine terms refers to the evaporation of wine through wood, or rather, a wooden barrel. When wine is stored in a barrel a proportion does evaporate through the pores of the wood and consequently such barrels have to be topped up with the same wine periodically to 'allow for evaporation'.

Exhibiting
Competitions are well worth entering, but be careful that you exhibit your bottle correctly. Whatever the colour of the wine the bottle should be of clear glass. The cork should be of the stopper variety because the bottle will be opened for tasting. The wine itself must be absolutely brilliant, not just clear. The points that are judged are usually: Flavour and Balance; Bouquet or Aroma; Clarity and Colour; Presentation.

Extracting juice
Some of the soft fruits (banana, strawberry, etc.) are impossible to press for juice and any attempts to do

so usually end with a soggy pulp. In this case you can only crush, mash or liquidize the fruit to add to the must. Other fruits such as grape and orange easily produce juice.

But it must be pointed out that it is not always advisable to make wine from juice alone. Oranges, for instance, are better off without their skins, while grapes and many other fruits have their flavour enhanced by the inclusion of tannins and other ingredients present in the skins. However, even when the whole fruit is used in the aerobic fermentation a press of some sort is useful so that the maximum amount of liquid—and consequently wine—is strained into the fermenting jar.

Extracts   These are concentrated essences that are added to wine to ensure a specific flavour; for instance, Vermouth or a variety of liqueurs. (See *Liqueurs*.)

F

Feeding   To achieve a high alcohol content in any wine without resorting to artificially adding alcohol, it is necessary to 'feed' the yeast. This is done by adding, or feeding, the sugar into the must in small quantities over a period. The reason for this is that if you add a large quantity of sugar at the outset the yeast will tire or 'stick' at, perhaps, 13 per cent alcohol or lower. However, if the sugar is added a bit at a time the yeast can cope better and, with a good yeast, could even reach a percentage of 21 per cent—the approximate strength of Port and Sherry.

You really need a hydrometer to carry out feeding accurately although even feeding sugar at, say, 25 per cent of the final amount every three weeks or so will create a higher strength than you would other-wise achieve. If you have a hydrometer, add 25 per cent of the sugar initially, and another 25 per cent when the hydrometer reading indicates there is only

Fennel

a few degrees of sugar left. Continue this until all the sugar has been added. (See *Hydrometer*.)

A herb more usually added to sauces or for making fennel tea, but it does make good wine. Be careful you don't use too much or a rather peculiar taste creeps through.

Fennel wine (dry)

Fennel leaves or small packet of dried	$\frac{1}{2}$ lb
Chopped apple	2 lb
Sugar	$2\frac{1}{2}$ lb
Citric acid	$\frac{1}{2}$ oz
Campden tablet	1
Yeast: All Purpose	
Water	1 gallon
Nutrient	

Method A. Aerobic fermentation for three days.

Fermentation

A complex process which never causes any amazement to the country farmer who makes his own wine, because he just gets on with the job of making wine without bothering about the chemical computations.

In simple terms, alcoholic fermentation is the conversion of sugar into alcohol and carbon dioxide. This it does on an approximate 50–50 basis—some of this is explained in Section One. However, it is not quite as simple as that. By-products are produced which somewhat reduce the proportion of alcohol such as glycerol (which is beneficial), succinic acid, esters, acids containing nitrogen (called amino acids) and, if you are very unlucky or careless, you could even end up with *acetobacter*. The whole process is precipitated by *enzymes*, and without these there would be no fermentation.

Fermentation is greatly affected by temperature. If it is too low (under 50°F or 10°C) the fermentation will stop or never start; if it is too high (over 90°F or 38°C) the yeast will die. An ideal temperature for starting a fermentation is around 75°F or 25°C.

Although a fermentation will eventually start with merely the addition of yeast to the must, it is preferable to add the yeast already working by means of a

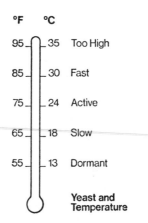

°F	°C	
95	35	Too High
85	30	Fast
75	24	Active
65	18	Slow
55	13	Dormant

Yeast and Temperature

starter bottle. Although the yeast will perform its job quickest when the must is fairly warm, this does not always produce the best wine. A heavily flavoured wine such as Bilberry or Black Currant can often get away with a quick 'hot' fermentation, but for more delicately flavoured wines such as the flower variety the best method is to ferment at a relatively low temperature. It will take longer, but it will not destroy the flavour.

(See also under *Strength* for alcoholic content, and Section One.)

Fig One of the finest dried fruits for winemaking. It has the particularly desirable characteristic of absorbing and retaining the flavour and balance of the particular yeast used—so make sure you don't waste this asset; use the best wine yeast. In common with most dried fruits, figs have a high sulphite content coating the outside to inhibit bacteria. This must be removed by washing thoroughly. Then any micro-organisms can be eliminated by boiling in the water for a quarter of an hour.

Fig wine (*semi-sweet*)

Washed, chopped dry figs	2 lb
Brown sugar	2½ lb
Citric acid	1 oz
Depectinizer	½ oz
Water	1 gallon
Yeast: Sherry	
Nutrient	

Method C. But keep the figs and water on the boil for fifteen minutes. Aerobic fermentation four days.

Filtration

The best way of obtaining a perfectly clear wine is to rack it and leave all traces of sediment behind, but, although this will often happen, sometimes the wine will not clear and there is no option but to filter or resort to fining.

Filtration is not necessarily an alternative to fining —one can be more suitable than the other for specific cases, filtering being the safer method in the case of suspended solids and fining essential if the cloudiness is a colloidal haze. If you are in doubt about which method to adopt, pour a small amount through a Whatman No. 1 paper filter. If the wine comes through clear you may safely filter, but if it is still cloudy the haze is colloidal and fining will have to be carried out.

Filtration is best carried out by means of fine cloth gauzes, which should be well rinsed to avoid any cloth taint, or through a paper filter. The latter unfortunately takes a long time and aerates the wine too much. Asbestos pulp has been frequently used in the past as a filter medium, but it definitely taints the wine, so it is best placed in its proper perspective —history.

The commercial producer has fewer problems because he has large filter plants at his disposal. In the past it has not been possible for the amateur winemaker to afford such a plant, but at the time of writing at least two filter units for the amateur

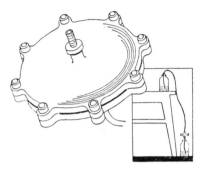

have come on the market. (The illustration shows the Vinbrite filter unit.) These units claim such a complete filtration that the wine is virtually stable afterwards. No doubt by the time you read this a filtration unit will have become a standard part of the serious winemaker's equipment. (See also *Fining*.)

Fining

When filtration is unsuccessful you will have to resort to fining. This is carried out by introducing another substance which has the effect of depositing the haze at the bottom of the container. You then simply rack off, but you will lose a little wine because fining agents leave a much thicker sediment behind.

One danger must be pointed out at the beginning, and that is the one of over-fining. If you add too much fining agent you will be left with not merely a haze but one of twice the density you started with. So be careful and, if in doubt, use too little rather than too much.

There are several substances you can use to fine, and they are all described under their headings, which are: *Egg white*, *Bentonite*, *Carbon* and *Casein* (neither of which should be used by the amateur), *Isinglass*, *Gelatine* and *Milk*.

Flaming

A technique used when yeast is cultivated on an agar slope in a test tube. A flame is held over the mouth of the test tube while the stopper is removed and replaced so as to ensure the minimum possible access by bacteria.

Flatness   Applied to sparkling wines, this means that it has lost its sparkle. In still wines it denotes a shortage of acid, which tends to make a wine unattractive and dull.

Flavour   We all know what flavour means in terms of our own preferences, and this is how a wine should be described when you refer to flavour. If the wine tastes like raspberry juice, then that is how the flavour should be described. There is a great difference between *flavour, aroma* and *bouquet*.

Flavouring   It is not usual for the flavour of the fruit or other ingredient to carry into the wine. Have you ever tasted a commercial wine that had the flavour of grape? On the other hand, sometimes it does. Strawberry and Raspberry wines will taste quite strongly of the fruit while other fruit flavours will not come through with even a hint. Orange and lemon juices can make nice wines without the faintest resemblance to the parent fruit—but if a little of the skin (without the white pith which is too bitter) is added the flavour of orange or lemon will be quite strong.

Flavouring extracts are a different matter and are dealt with under *Liqueurs*.

'Flogger'   See *Corking tools*.

Flor   Spanish word for flower. In wine terms it means an unusual and special yeast native to the Sherry country. It forms a white film or 'flower' on the surface of the wines and gives Sherry its characteristic taste.

Flower wines Most flowers heads will make an attractive wine, but the flavour in general is delicate and can be destroyed by boiling water. For this reason with flower wines it is better to infuse with cold water and rely on Campden or similar sterilizing agents to eliminate bacteria.

Folly   A wine made from the prunings or green tendrils of a grape vine. Well worth trying if you grow grapes— or know someone who does!

Folly, or Vine wine (dry)

Vine leaves and tendrils	5 lb
Sugar	$2\frac{1}{4}$ lb
Citric acid	$\frac{1}{2}$ oz
Water	1 gallon
Yeast: Bordeaux	
Nutrient	

Method B. Aerobic fermentation three days.

Fortification The adding of alcohol to a wine to either arrest fermentation and leave some unfermented sugar, or to give better keeping properties or to make the wine stronger.

A neutral spirit such as Vodka or Polish white spirit should be used, but Brandy can be used if a Sherry- or Port-style wine is being attempted.

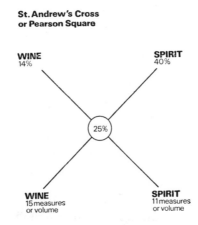

St. Andrew's Cross
or Pearson Square

You will need to assess the final alcohol content before you start and this is easily done by means of a Pearson Square or St Andrew's Cross. You draw a diagonal cross as illustrated. In the centre you write the required percentage of your fortified wine. At the top-left corner you write the percentage of alcohol in the wine to be fortified and at the top-right you place the percentage of alcohol in the spirit or fortifying liquid. Then you deduct the figure at the top-left from the figure in the middle and place the answer at the bottom-right. Then deduct the figure in the middle from the figure at top-right and place the answer in the bottom-left. You then read off from the bottom two figures from left to right in terms of measures or volume. Thus in our illustration we find that if we have a 14 per cent wine and a 40 per cent spirit and we want to bring the percentage of the final product to 25 per cent, then we must combine each fifteen measures of wine with eleven measures of spirit.

Fructose   When yeast starts to ferment household sugar, it first splits the sugar up into two components—glucose and fructose.

Fruit, Canned   See *Canned food*.

Fruit, Dried   It is not necessarily true to say that fresh fruit makes the best wine. In some cases a dried fruit produces an even better wine than the fresh variety. One case in point is the fig, which always seems to produce a wine with more body and richness when made from the dried fruit. Another favourable aspect about dried fruit is that usually it imposes less of the original fruit flavour on a wine and tends to adopt the flavour of a particular yeast to a greater extent. This means, for example, that if you are trying to make a Tokay-type wine from figs and tokay yeast, you are liable to be more successful with dried figs than fresh.

Apart from such as spin-dried raisins and sultanas, dried fruits are usually heavily coated with a sticky, sulphited mess which could retard fermentation and which in any case is not very appetizing, so they should be well washed in clean water before being chopped or minced for the must.

Because dried fruits usually harbour a lot of micro-organisms, method C should be employed whenever possible. Where such as dried apricots are used, boiling will produce a gummy haze that is often difficult to clear and in these cases methods A or B should be used, but be sure to sterilize with Campden or something similar before proceeding with the fermentation.

Dried fruits are reduced to approximately 25 per cent of their original volume, and this must be taken into account when formulating recipes. One measure of dried fruit is equal to approximately four measures of fresh.

Funnel A plastic funnel is the most popular, and probably the best. Make sure, however, that it is not too small. A 5-inch funnel is the best all-round article.

G

Galvanized Galvanized ware should never be used because zinc is dissolved by certain fruits to form soluble zinc salts, which are poisonous.

Gelatine A fining agent that can remove even tannin and colouring to a certain extent. Because of this it is normal to add only half the estimated quantity first to avoid overfining. Use B.P. grade gelatine, or the purest available. It can be seen how easy it is to overfine by the quantity ($\frac{1}{64}$ oz) of gelatine required for each gallon of wine; working with such small quantities it is very easy to make a mistake.

Ginger Most often used as an additional flavouring. If you like the taste of ginger and you have access to a large amount of cheap fruit that you are not keen on when made into wine—then add some crushed root ginger to the must.

Ginger wine (dry)

Crushed root ginger	1 oz
Strong tea	$\frac{1}{2}$ pint
Sugar	$2\frac{1}{2}$ lb
Citric acid	$\frac{1}{4}$ oz
Water	1 gallon

Yeast: All Purpose
Nutrient

Method C. Aerobic fermentation two days.

Glass   Despite its fragility, just about the best material for
the production of wine, from the must to the bottle,
with the exception of an oak barrel during the pre-
bottling period. Glass can be sterilized easily and,
almost as important, you can see exactly what is
going on. This is most important when racking.

Providing it is clean, glass cannot impart any 'off'
flavours, and this cannot be said of most plastics or
other materials.

Glasses   You can of course drink wine out of a cup, but there
is no doubt that an attractive glass improves the
enjoyment of a good brilliant wine. There is a wide
variety of glass shapes, but we will not dwell upon
them here. We should know something, however,
about glasses that might mar our enjoyment.

Glasses should be incurved, so that the aroma
and/or bouquet can be appreciated; for the same
reason, never fill a glass more than two-thirds
full.

Wash glasses in detergent to remove all traces of
grease, and rinse thoroughly in fresh water. If there
is anything worse than a greasy glass for sampling
wine, it is detergent residue.

Glazes   Earthenware utensils are often very useful for the
production of wine. However, you should make sure
the glaze is hard. It is rare that you will find a soft
glaze nowadays (test with your fingernail to check
whether it's soft or hard), but if you do, don't use it.
There is every possibility that such a glaze would
contain lead.

Gloegg   A traditional Swedish Christmas drink composed of
red wine, almonds, gin, cinnamon, cloves and raisins
in varying proportions.

Glucose   Technically, a monosaccharide hexose sugar. From
our point of view this is just another sugar which can

be used in place of the household variety except that it is more expensive.

Glycerine If wine is too dry and you do not wish to add sugar, or if the wine is astringent due to a surfeit of tannin, then glycerine may help to improve the former or mask (but not cure) the latter.

Half an ounce should be added to each pint of wine.

Glycerol A by-product of the fermentation process, glycerol assists in adding smoothness to the flavour of a wine.

It is worth noting that the popular mould inhibitor sulphur dioxide, which is widely used in winemaking, can also inhibit the glycerol content of a wine—and hence its smoothness.

Golden rod A late-flowering border plant that grows in profusion. Excellent for the production of wine, the flower heads only should be used. Use the recipe and method as for *Broom wine*.

Gooseberry One of the finest fruits for the production of a white wine. Properly made it can produce wine with an uncanny resemblance to Hock or Chablis, but I prefer it made just as . . . Gooseberry wine. It is low in tannin, high in acid and needs a depectinizer to ensure that the final product will be bright.

Gooseberry wine (dry)

Squashed ripe gooseberries	6 lb
Sugar	2½ lb
Depectinizer	½ oz
Tannin	pinch
Water	1 gallon
Yeast: Chablis	
Nutrient	

Method B. Aerobic fermentation four days.

Gorse Some say this is the finest flower wine. Use the recipe and method as for *Broom wine*, but reduce the amount of sugar by ½ lb.

Grape The original, and some say the only, wine. For

thousands of years man has made wine from grape and so, we assume, it must be the finest fruit from which to make wine. This is incorrect. Grape has always been the most popular fruit for winemaking for the simple reason that it generally contains the correct proportions of sugar, acid, tannin, yeast (on the skin) and other ingredients. So all one really has to do is squash the grapes, leave for a few days and presto! wine! Is it any wonder that the grape has been so popular? If, say, it were plums and not grapes that held these magic ingredients, then the plum would hold the esteemed position the grape now has, despite the entirely different taste.

Grape concentrate

Concentrated grape juice is becoming popular among winemakers. There is no fiddly squashing, crushing or chopping of fruit; just dilute and add yeast and (sometimes) sugar, and no more need be done until racking time. It is certainly a means of producing a reasonable bottle of grape wine at a reasonable price.

The concentrate sold in winemaking shops always has the recipe and procedure on the label, or available in a leaflet.

Grapefruit

While capable of producing a really excellent wine, the grapefruit is very high in acid and low in sugar, so the juice must be diluted with water and extra sugar added. Be careful about the skin. While the pulp flesh can be added to the must without fear, or the bright yellow exterior of the peel may be lightly grated into the must to give a stronger grapefruit flavour, the fleshy white pith in the peel must on no account be added, otherwise you will be faced with an impossibly bitter wine.

Grapefruit wine (dry)

6 large grapefruit	
Sugar	2½ lb
Depectinizer	½ oz
Water up to	1 gallon

Yeast: Bernkastler
Nutrient

The grapefruit must be peeled and the skin thrown away. The segments are then sliced finely. Method B. Aerobic fermentation three days.

Greengage A popular fruit that makes an excellent wine. Use the method and recipe as for *Damson wine*, but substitute a Sauterne yeast.

Guava This makes a very agreeable wine. It is a tropical fruit not widely sold in Britain, so the best method is to use canned fruit. For recipe, see Section Three.

Gums Carbohydrates of a very complicated nature, gums are always formed to some extent during fermentation. It is normally no problem to the winemaker, but some dried fruits, especially apricots, tend to give off additional amounts of gum, making the wine difficult to clear. For this reason one should not boil dried fruits for very long if they are being used for making wine.

Gypsum Calcium sulphate (plaster of Paris). In Spain a certain amount is added to Sherry must to improve the texture and add acidity.

H

Harshness See *Astringent*.

Hawthorn Or Crataegus. A plant that has been used as an impenetrable hedge for centuries. Both the flowers and berries make excellent, distinctive wine.

Hawthorn Berry wine (medium)

Crushed hawthorn berries	6 lb
Sugar	3 lb
Citric acid	½ oz
Water	1 gallon
Yeast: Hock	
Nutrient	

Method B. Aerobic fermentation three days.

Hawthorn Blossom wine (dry)

Use recipe and method as for *Burnet wine*, but reduce quantity of blossom to half a gallon.

Hazes
There are broadly two types of wine haze. The colloidal, which requires fining, and suspended solids, which can be filtered. (See *Filtration*.)

Heat
Heat can be used for sterilizing wine utensils, but this is a laborious method, and most winemakers prefer to use chemicals such as sulphite.

Of more direct value is the knowledge that heat is required for fermentation; further, that too much heat will kill a fermentation, and too little will stop it. (See also *Fermentation*; *Iron*; *Pectin*; *Starch*.)

Herbs
Herbs have been used to impart various flavours to wines from time immemorial. They are used in part to produce flavouring essences for Vermouth and other apéritif wines, and you can do the same if you wish.

Herbs are also useful if the wine you have made is not quite to your taste, and you don't fancy infusing it with spices such as cinnamon or ginger.

Two ounces (no more) of aromatic herbs can be (*a*) added to the must or (*b*) suspended in a fine linen bag either in the fermenting liquid or in the wine prior to racking. This is for 1 gallon of liquid.

Hock
From Germany, one of the world's great white wines. (See Section Three.)

Honey
An excellent medium that can be used in place of sugar. However, it is not as neutral as sugar. Honey will always have a slight background flavour of the original flower it was derived from, and so is better employed in making one of the oldest drinks known (see *Mead*).

It is important to note that honey contains approximately 25 per cent water, so that four parts of honey contains only three parts fermentable sugar. This is important if you are using honey in a recipe instead of sugar.

Honeysuckle   The fragrant flowers of this plant make a delightful dry wine. It also makes a good sweet wine but somehow the delicate flavour is lost in the sweetness.

Honeysuckle wine (dry)

Use recipe and method as for *Burnet wine*, but use a Hock yeast instead and only half a gallon of flowers.

Hops   Better known in association with beer, hops can in fact make a rather unusual wine which, while not to everybody's taste, might well suit you.

Hop wine (medium)

Hops	3 oz
Minced raisins	8 oz
Sugar	2½ lb
Citric acid	½ oz
Water	1 gallon
Yeast: Bordeaux	
Nutrient	

Method B. Aerobic fermentation four days.

Huckleberry   Another name for *Bilberry*.

Hydrometer   The instrument for the serious winemaker. Don't fall into the trap of thinking the hydrometer is a difficult instrument to operate. Used basically it can be operated by a child to assess whether a must will finish as a dry or sweet wine; and tell you when the fermentation is virtually finished.

First of all let's assess what a hydrometer is designed for. For our purpose it measures the amount of sugar in a liquid. Thus we can tell at the outset whether the final wine will be sweet or dry. Also, when the hydrometer indicates there is no sugar left, the fermentation for all practical purposes is over.

The hydrometer is a glass tube with a bulbous, weighted end, containing a scale along its length. When it is immersed in the liquid the hydrometer will float higher as the proportion of sugar is increased.

Conversely, the less sugar in the liquid the deeper the hydrometer will sink. As the amount of sugar in the original liquid is converted into approximately 50 per cent alcohol, the scale at the side can be converted to give you the approximate percentage of alcohol in the finished wine.

All hydrometers sold have instructions included on how to use them. Assuming that you have a hydrometer produced for winemaking (they make them for other purposes), at one point farthest from the bulb end you will see a reading of 1·000. This is the 'zero' figure in relation to sugar. At 1·000 there is virtually no sugar present. At readings below this, i.e. 0·980, the indication will be that there is in fact slightly more alcohol present. Readings higher than 1·000 indicate the proportion of sugar. For an eventual dry wine an initial reading should be around 1·088 after sugar, if any, has been added. This will give you a wine of approximately 12 per cent alcohol. For a sweet wine the initial reading should be 1·130 or higher, although to save possible disaster it is better to stick to 1·130 and add more sugar when the reading has dropped to 1·000 or below.

Readings are taken in a tall, slim hydrometer jar.

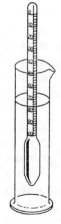

NB: In reading hydrometer scales, the first 1 and decimal point are sometimes omitted. Thus 10=1·010, 88=1·088, etc.

The beauty of a hydrometer is not only consistency of results—it also saves expensive guesswork. For instance, you might have a recipe that uses several pounds of raisins and other fruits. How can you assess how much sugar they contain? The only accurate way is to soak the fruit until all sugar is in solution and then use a hydrometer in the liquid.

Suspended matter can affect the readings, so make sure your test liquid is suitably free from this. Spin the hydrometer in the liquid before looking at it; bubbles clinging to the sides can also affect it.

Hydrometers are designed to be read when the liquid is at a temperature of 59°F (14°C). If the temperature varies from this the final reading will have to be adjusted. The correction if the temperature is slightly under is too small to worry about, but if it is higher: at 77°F add 2; at 95°F add 5.

The final alcoholic strength is assessed according to instructions given with each hydrometer, and as manufacturers sometimes use different systems to obtain the same estimation there is no point in explaining another here.

As a rough guide use the following for the must:

Dry wine — 1·088 to 1·095
Medium — 1·110 to 1·130
Sweet — 1·135 to 1·150

(See also *Specific gravity* and *Strength*.)

Hygiene
Cleanliness is all-important if you wish to avoid a succession of winemaking failures. Airborne bacteria can be kept at bay only by constantly keeping everything scrupulously clean and sterilized.

For a general sterilizing liquid make up a mixture of two Campden tablets and a spoonful of citric acid in a pint of water. This can be used to swill out utensils and wipe down equipment, or even to rinse your hands.

Hypocras
Pyment is wine made from grape juice and honey. Hypocras is spiced Pyment.

I

Improver   Any ingredient used to enhance a wine can be termed an improver. Glycerine added to a dry wine to sweeten it is an improver, as would be sugar, or gelatine added to fine a high concentration of tannin out of a wine. There are also proprietary improvers developed for various reasons.

It follows, then, that what might be an improver for one person is the very opposite for another, just as one person prefers sweet wine and the other prefers dry.

Indicator paper   A BDH Narrow Range pH indicator paper is a simple way of assessing the acid content of the must. It is not extremely accurate but is possibly near enough for the home winemaker.

Inoculating needle   An instrument used for removing a little yeast from an *agar* slope to make a starter, or to add to the must.

Insipid   Description of a wine lacking in 'bite'. This is usually the result of insufficient tannin.

Instant wine   This is the name given to a wine which is quickly made and quick to mature. It often uses a cereal or malt and/or fruit juice in place of time-consuming pulp. It must be devoid of excess tannin. There are very many recipes and most winemakers have their personal favourites.

Invert sugar   At the first stage of fermentation sugar is 'inverted' by the yeast, and splits into two sugar types, glucose and laevulose (fructose). Invert sugar is in fact already at this stage and as a result ferments quicker than ordinary sugar because one stage of the fermentation has already been completed. You can purchase invert sugar but it is more expensive and is useful only in certain cases. If you decide to use invert sugar, you should use 50 per cent more than ordinary household sugar (or three parts invert for every two parts household sugar).

Iodine solution   Dilute iodine solution is used to detect starch as the possible culprit of a haze. Even in small concentrations the wine will turn blue if iodine is added and starch is present (but the test sample should be thrown away after). Just add about six drops of tincture of iodine to half an egg-cup of wine. If the wine turns blue you will have to treat for starch, while a brown colour indicates that no starch is present.

Isinglass   Similar in action to gelatine and albumen, isinglass has the advantage over gelatine in that it is less easy to overfine. On the other hand, unless rigorously controlled conditions prevail, isinglass can be somewhat erratic. It must not be confused with the mineral isinglass.

J

Jam   Sometimes winemakers have access to bulk quantities of cheap jam. This of course provides both fruit and sugar, but it is essential to test the must with a hydrometer because the sugar content varies with different brands of jam. The essential point is to make sure that the jam contains only fruit and sugar. If preservatives are used it might be difficult or impossible to ferment. If an artificial sweetener is present it will not ferment out and you will be left with a sweet wine regardless.

Jelly bag   A filter bag for straining the wine thoroughly.

Judging   Judging wine beyond the simple 'I like it or I don't' principle requires experience and study. The basic guide-lines laid down for judging competitions (see *Exhibiting*) should be followed, because that is how others will judge *your* wines. There is also an excellent booklet on this very subject in the bibliography.

K

Kentish cup   A traditional cup consisting of ¼ Sherry, ¾ sweet Cider, grated rind and juice of orange, juice of lemon, and a dash of angostura bitters just before serving well chilled.

Kloeckera apiculatus An apiculate or wild yeast. It is rather inefficient in converting sugar to alcohol and cannot produce a wine with keeping qualities because it is killed by alcohol in quantities greater than 5·5 per cent.

Kohl rabi Sometimes used as a substitute for turnips; but, establishing itself as a vegetable in its own right, I find the resultant wine a little characterless, but quite good if sweet.

Kohl Rabi wine (sweet)

Minced kohl rabi	4 lb
Sugar	3½ lb
Citric acid	½ oz
Tannin	pinch
Water	1 gallon
Yeast: Sauterne	
Nutrient	

Method C. Aerobic fermentation four days.

L

Labelling Apart from looking decorative and efficient, the most important aspect of a label is that it provides essential information. To do this the label must contain (a) the name of the winemaker, (b) the ingredient(s), (c) whether the wine is sweet, dry or in-between, (d) the month and year it ceased fermenting and (e) the winemaker's bin or batch number, so that full details of production can be looked up in the log-book.

Every winemaker will be able to complete the first four items, and the last one obviously requires enough dedication to keep records.

Don't fall into the misleading habit of describing a wine which, for instance, contains parsnip and raisins as 'Parsnip wine'—the correct title is 'Parsnip and Raisin'. Too many winemakers title the wine according to what they consider to be the main ingredient. This is very confusing.

Lactobacilli   See *Malo-lactic*.

Laevulose   A sugar produced during the first stage of fermentation. (See also *Invert sugar*.)

Lavender   I must confess to failure here. Although I have tasted quite passable wines that were allegedly Lavender wines, I have never made even a passable wine out of the plant without adding lots of raisins or other ingredients. As such, they were not really Lavender wines and therefore outside the purpose of this book. I would also suggest that in the light of my own experience lavender on its own does not produce a worthwhile wine.

Lees   The deposit of yeast and/or sediment formed at the bottom of a fermenting or storage vessel, or at the bottom of a bottle of wine.

Legal position   We are talking here about home winemaking. The position varies in different countries, but in Britain the situation at the time of writing is that you can make as much wine at home as you like, provided it is only for the consumption of yourself and your friends. *But not a drop must be sold*. The same applies to beer.

Distilling, in any shape or form, is strictly illegal —and dangerous.

Lemon   Lemon is a very acid fruit and, as such, requires a high degree of dilution to make a palatable wine. Unfortunately such a high dilution renders the finished wine rather weak and characterless. The only way round this is to make sure that the finished wine *tastes* of lemon. To ensure this, the finely grated rind of one lemon (*without* the white pith) should be added to the must in the proportion of one lemon per gallon.

Lemon wine (dry)

Juice of 8 lemons
Grated lemon rind

Sugar	2½ lb
Campden tablet	1
Tannin	pinch
Water	1 gallon
Yeast: Champagne	
Nutrient	

Method A. Aerobic fermentation two days.

Lemon thyme A prolific herb with a lemon scent. It makes a rather delicious wine and, although I quote a basic recipe, I think it is even better if 1 lb of minced sultanas is added and the sugar reduced to 2 lb.

Lemon Thyme wine (dry)

Use recipe and method as for *Burnet wine*, but use only 1 pint of lemon thyme leaves (no stalks) in place of burnet flowers, and substitute a Hock yeast.

Light Light, and especially sunlight, has a detrimental effect on wine. Although ultra-violet light hastens ageing it is an unpredictable process and wines are best left to ferment and mature in the dark. Red wine particularly can lose a great deal of its colour if continually exposed to light.

Lime The section on *Lemon* applies equally to lime, including the wine and method.

Liqueurs After a fine meal there is little better—or more expensive—than a fine liqueur. However, expense is of only secondary concern to the home winemaker because most of the great liqueurs can be imitated with reasonable success by the careful use of wine, spirit and commercial extracts or herbs.

Roughly, the procedure is to prepare a blend of neutral wine (cereal is best), and 140° proof spirit to the strength required, sweeten with sugar syrup, shake, then add the flavouring. (To assess the strength, see the Pearson Square under *Fortification*.)

Liquidizing The liquidizer is an excellent way of preparing ingredients for a wine must if the amounts are not too great. However, when the ingredients contain skins rich in tannin such as elderberry or sloe, the aerobic fermentation will release more tannin than the crushed fruit would. In such cases it is best to cut the aerobic fermentation short by one day, otherwise the wine will need gelatine fining or long ageing.

Loganberry Makes an excellent wine. Use the recipe and method as for *Blackberry wine.*

Log-books An essential requirement if your results are to be consistent; a well-kept log-book is also a nostalgic reminder of your winemaking past and heroic experiments!

A good log-book should have space for inserts as to: the variety of the wine; the ingredients; specific gravity of must; yeast variety; nutrient; any other ingredients (improvers, etc.); the date fermentation commenced; the date fermentation finished; dates of rackings; any other additions; bottling date with specific gravity at that time; approximate alcohol content; any remarks; bin or batch number.

Loquat A fruit that is more usually found in tins—so that is the basis for our recipe.

Loquat wine (sweet)

14-oz tins of loquats	4
Sugar	3 lb
Citric acid	½ oz
Water	1 gallon
Yeast: Sauterne	
Nutrient	

Method A. Aerobic fermentation four days.

Lovage A herb that is not as popular as it was. The leaves make, I think, an indifferent wine unless other ingredients are added. But then, of course, it is no longer pure Lovage wine. However, if you have an abundance of lovage it is always worth a try. Use the recipe and method as for *Broom wine*, but replace the broom flowers with 1½ lb lovage.

M

Madeira	See Section Three.
Mahonia	Or Oregon grape. A decorative shrub, the berries should be picked only when they are blue and white right through and after the first good frost.

Use the recipe and method as for *Black Currant*, but increase the fruit content to 5 lb and use a Hock yeast.

I must confess that I have never tried this wine—I have never had enough berries—but a friend of mine assures me it is excellent.

Malo-lactic Malic acid is found in apples and other fruits. Sometimes a certain anaerobic bacteria will commence to convert the malic acid into lactic acid, which is much less acid. The result of this—the malo-lactic fermentation—gives a slight sparkle to the wine which some people are fond of. Others, however, try to avoid it.

The result of a malo-lactic fermentation is certainly a fresh taste and I personally am grateful if it occurs.

Malt More usually associated with beer, malt makes a good and slightly unusual wine; and of course it is available all the year round. I must point out that we are referring here to plain malt extract, and not the variety with added cod liver oil!

Malt wine (medium)

Malt extract	1 lb
Sugar	3 lb
Citric acid	½ oz
Water up to	1 gallon
Yeast: Tarragona or Port	
Nutrient	

Method B. Place in fermentation jar under air lock as soon as fermentation commences.

Marigold There are several varieties of marigold, and I assume that they are all similar from the aspect of making wine. However, I can vouch that the following recipe, made from dwarf French marigolds, produces an attractive dry wine.

Marigold wine (dry)

Marigold flowers	3 quarts
Sugar	2½ lb
Citric acid	½ oz
Campden tablet	1
Water	1 gallon
Yeast: Hock	
Nutrient	

Method A. Aerobic fermentation four days.

Marrow   Personally I find that plain Marrow wine is rather insipid—but I hasten to add that there are plenty who disagree with me. I find demerara sugar goes best with Marrow and, if you find it still insipid, an ounce of root ginger powder in the must will work wonders and make it quite an attractive drink.

Marrow wine (sweet)

Ripe marrow flesh, chopped	5 lb
Demerara sugar	3½ lb
Citric acid	½ oz
Depectinizer	½ oz
Water up to	1 gallon
Yeast: Malaga or Sherry	
Nutrient	

Method B. Aerobic fermentation three days.

Marrow rum   A rather exotic-sounding beverage which is usually a sweet, gooey let-down. But it is fun to do and perhaps you will like it better than I do, especially if you have a sweet tooth.

Obtain a fair-sized marrow with a tough, un-bruised skin and cut one end off a few inches below the stalk end. Scoop out the middle where the seeds are and fill the cavity with demerara sugar. Mix a little yeast with some acid (lemon or grapefruit) fruit juice and pour this over the sugar. The stalk 'top' must now be replaced and sealed with adhesive tape and the marrow hung in a warm place. In a few weeks liquid will start to seep out. At this point punch a fair-sized hole in the bottom of the marrow and let it drip into a small fermentation jar. When no more liquid is coming out fit an air lock and ferment out.

This 'rum' is best aged for at least nine months, and served cold.

Maturation   The same as *Ageing*.

Mead   Probably the oldest wine, Mead is made simply from honey and water. It is a wine that some like and some don't. But it is true to say that it is often temperamental in production unless you specialize mainly in Mead and know its behaviour. For instance, it is likely to stick during fermentation.

There is one unusual aspect of Mead. If, say, orange juice is made into wine the resultant liquid tastes not at all like orange. However, a Mead made from orange-blossom honey will, if unblended, have a background taste of orange. This applies in general, so be careful what type of honey you use.

The best Mead is made from very pale honey derived from a single flower—blends can produce a peculiar flavour. (See also *Honey*.)

Mead (dry)

Honey	$3\frac{1}{4}$ lb
Citric acid	$\frac{3}{4}$ oz
Tannin	$\frac{1}{2}$ teaspoon
Campden tablet	1
Water up to	1 gallon
Yeast: Mead	
Nutrient	

Method A. Place in fermenting jar and fit air lock as soon as fermentation commences.

This recipe is designed for a Mead that must age for at least a year. For quicker drinking omit the tannin and reduce the acid to ½ oz.

Meadow-sweet One of the most attractive wild flowers, generally distributed in wet meadows and near water. The flavour is rather delicate and so a lot of flowers are needed to make a suitable wine. Use the recipe and method as for *Broom wine*.

Medlar An ancient fruit (even Shakespeare mentioned it), the medlar has never been popular, although it was once considered a good partner to Port. Picked about November, the fruit should be so ripe as to be soft before eating or making into wine.

Medlar wine (*medium*)

Squashed medlars	6 lb
Sugar	3 lb
Citric acid	¼ oz
Tannin	pinch
Depectinizer	½ oz
Water	1 gallon
Yeast: Burgundy	
Nutrient	

Method B. Aerobic fermentation four days.

Melomel A wine made from honey and any fruit except apples (*Cyser*) or grape (*Pyment*).

Metal Various metals such as galvanized iron or iron and copper will ruin a wine. Avoid using any metal vessel or instrument in winemaking with the exception of aluminium (for boiling but not fermenting); stainless steel can be used for just about anything; enamel ware is fine providing it is not chipped at all.

Micro-organisms See *Bacteria*, *Yeast* and *Moulds*. These are all micro-organisms—some of them essential, and some of them we try to avoid.

Milk This contains casein and as such is a rather useful fining medium and, especially, a decolouring medium.

For this purpose, prepare three or four small clear

bottles with about 100 cc (each) of the wine. To the first bottle add ½ cc of milk, to the second 1 cc and then 1½ cc. Shake the bottles and stand for thirty-six hours. Select the colour that suits you and you have the correct measure on hand.

Mint   Useful to use as an added ingredient for evolving unusual wines, mint does not make a very nice wine on its own. However, in combination with tea it does provide a rather fascinating drink.

Mint and Tea wine (*sweet*)

Bruised mint leaves	1½ pints
Strong tea	½ pint
Citric acid	½ oz
Water	1 gallon
Yeast: All Purpose	
Nutrient	

Method B. Aerobic fermentation two days.

Morat   An Anglo-Saxon drink. (See Section Three.)
Morello   See *Cherry*.
Moulds   Micro-organisms which produce cotton-like threads called mycellium. Moulds are airborne and as such need to be guarded against. Sterile utensils are a prevention, but not entirely. Sometimes when a fermentation is slow in starting a mould will grow on the surface of the must. This is no great problem if caught early; just spoon the mould off and get the fermentation going quickly. From this aspect alone a 'starter' is the best bet for getting a fermentation going.

Mountain Ash   Or Rowan. An elegant tree up to 30 feet high. The fruits are like little red apples and are soon eaten by birds—and as it is the fruit you need for the wine you have to be quick about it.

Rowanberry (*Mountain Ash*) *wine* (*sweet*)

Squashed rowan berries	5 lb
Sugar	3½ lb

Citric acid	$\frac{1}{4}$ oz
Water	1 gallon
Yeast: Bordeaux	
Nutrient	

Method C. Aerobic fermentation four days.

Mousiness   Or ropiness, or oiliness. A condition where the wine takes on an appearance like egg white and pours like treacle. It may appear in rope-like coils. This is the work of a lactic acid bacteria. The taste remains relatively unaffected.

The cure: Whip the wine into a froth, adding two Campden tablets per gallon. Filter. After three weeks rack off any sediment that may have accumulated. With a little luck no one will ever tell that there had been anything amiss. (See also *Musty.*)

Mulberry   This tree was introduced to Britain long before Shakespeare's time; in fact the Anglo-Saxons used to produce their favourite drink—*Morat*—from the fruit. It makes an excellent wine. Use the recipe and method as for *Bilberry wine.*

Must   This is the liquid and pulp of basic ingredients from which a wine is made.

Musty   When a wine smells musty it is sometimes called 'mousy', which serves to confuse it with oiliness, etc. However, in this case it is caused by *Autolysis.*

Mycellium   See *Moulds.*

N

Nectarine   A smaller, smooth-skinned version of the peach. Produces a good white wine. Use the recipe and method as for *Peach wine.*

Nettle   The young nettle tops are used for this wine, but even at its best it is lacking in character. For my own use I would add $\frac{1}{2}$ oz of root ginger powder to each gallon of must, but first try it without.

Nettle wine (*sweet*)

Bruised young nettle tops	3 quarts
Sugar	3½ lb
Citric acid	¼ oz
Water	1 gallon
Yeast: Hock	
Nutrient	

Method B. Aerobic fermentation five days.

Nitrogen   Yeast cells need nitrogen to multiply. Although fruit juices contain some nitrogen, when diluted there is usually not sufficient for a satisfactory fermentation. For this reason ammonium salts (sulphate or phosphate) are usually added as these contain a rich source of nitrogen. The salts are conveniently sold as Yeast Nutrient.

Nose   Wine tasters' term for bouquet or aroma. It is a neutral word (like 'taste') and does not suggest superiority.

Nutrient   A yeast 'food', or energizer. It supplies the must with a suitable source of Nitrogen.

Nylon   A nylon mesh or strainer is a useful item of winemaking equipment. It can be washed and sterilized easily and does not taint the wine.

O

Oak   The supreme wood for wine barrels. All the really fine red wines in the world owe part of their quality to ageing in oak barrels. A new oak barrel will often make the wine very astringent due to an excessive infusion of tannin. This means that the wine must be kept longer so that the tannin is mellowed—and this helps make a finer wine.

Some winemakers add oak sawdust to the must if it is lacking in tannin. But now that tannin in powder form is readily available this is completely unnecessary.

Oak leaf   The oak leaf makes a fair to middling wine. I can't say that I recommend it, but oak leaves are cheap, it makes a good talking point and you might even like it!

Oak Leaf wine (*sweet*)

Oak leaves	1 gallon
Sugar	$3\frac{1}{2}$ lb
Citric acid	$\frac{1}{2}$ oz
Water	1 gallon
Yeast: Hock	
Nutrient	

Method B. Aerobic fermentation one day only. The one-day fermentation applies only if you are using a 'starter' and fermentation gets under way immediately. If you just want to add the yeast to the must, then infuse the leaves overnight, strain and when fermenting pour into fermentation jar and fit air lock.

Oiliness   See *Mousiness.*

Off flavours These are listed under their respective names (*Acetic Acid, Musty,* etc.).

Onion   I have tried wine made from only onions. It was lacking in character and almost tasteless. I have tried a similar wine with the addition of raisins—and it tasted like Raisin wine. So I am forced to assume that a pure Onion wine is not worth making except to amuse yourself with, and as it seems to add little to other wines it is a waste of time using it as an additional ingredient.

Orange   Makes a superb white wine. If carefully produced it can be indistinguishable from a good commercial grape white wine. Because of bitter ingredients in the pith of oranges it is best to make the wine from the juice. Make sure that the oranges are nice and sweet, If they are acid the quantity of juice can be reduced by up to a half.

Orange wine (dry)

Orange juice	2 pints
Sugar	2½ lb
Tannin	½ teaspoon
Water	6 pints
Yeast: Chablis or Hock	
Nutrient	

Mix all ingredients together. As soon as fermentation commences, pour into fermentation jar and fit air lock. If a sweet wine is required, increase sugar to 3½ lb and omit tannin.

Oregon grape   See *Mahonia*.

Oxidation   Many fruits start to go brown through oxidation as soon as they are exposed to air—or, rather, oxygen. The same can happen to wines that have been exposed to air, such as by excessive racking. The wine then starts to darken and this is of course particularly noticeable with white wines. If this should happen, add two Campden tablets per gallon to the wine to stabilize it.

Oxygen   Apart from its action in *oxidation*, the part oxygen plays in winemaking is via its presence—or absence—during the fermentation. Wine yeast needs oxygen for reproduction only. Deprive it of oxygen and it will cease to multiply but continue converting the sugar into alcohol. This is another good reason for excluding air by means of the air lock, because we do not seek a large colony of yeast, but merely to convert what sugar there is.

P

Pansy   Popular in the garden—and useful as a wine.

Pansy wine (sweet)

Pansy flowers	½ gallon
Sugar	3½ lb

Citric acid	$\frac{1}{2}$ oz
Campden tablet	1
Water	1 gallon

Yeast: Tokay or Sauterne
Nutrient

Method A. Aerobic fermentation four days. If the resultant wine is lacking in body, add $\frac{1}{2}$ lb of minced sultanas to the next batch.

Parsley

Very popular as a country wine, and very good at that. Be careful not to add more than the recommended amount of parsley, otherwise the flavour becomes too pronounced and spoils the wine.

Parsley wine (dry)

Chopped parsley	1 lb
Sugar	$2\frac{1}{2}$ lb
Juice of two oranges	
Tannin	$\frac{1}{4}$ teaspoon
Water	1 gallon

Yeast: Chablis
Nutrient

Method B. Aerobic fermentation four days. If you fancy a sweet wine raise the sugar to $3\frac{1}{2}$ lb, omit the tannin and replace the yeast with Tokay.

Parsnip

An old favourite with the British home winemaker. It makes an excellent wine, but I think it is better sweet than dry.

Parsnip wine (sweet)

Chopped parsnip	4 lb
Sugar, brown	$3\frac{1}{2}$ lb
Citric acid	$\frac{1}{2}$ oz
Water	1 gallon

Yeast: Sherry or Burgundy
Nutrient

Method C. Aerobic fermentation five days. Some people add a small piece ($\frac{1}{2}$ oz) of root ginger to the

must. If you want a dry wine reduce the sugar to
2½ lb and substitute white, and add ¼ teaspoon of
tannin. Leave out the ginger.

Passion fruit   Also known as the Purple Granadilla. Technically
one of the Passiflora family, there are many varieties
and they produce fruit something like a plum—but
take heed, they are not all edible, and the edible ones
make the best wine. Use the recipe and method as
for Plum.

Pasteurization   This is a method of sterilizing the wine by heat treatment. The wine is heated up to 140°F, taking twenty
minutes to reach this temperature. This temperature
is held for twenty minutes, then the wine is allowed
to cool naturally. Although frequently used in com-
merce, pasteurization is too cumbersome a method
for the average winemaker, and undoubtedly makes
a slight difference to the flavour of the wine.

Paw-paw   A tropical fruit. (See Section Three.)

Peach   An excellent fruit that makes a really good white
wine from both the fresh or dried fruit.

Peach wine (dry)

Stoned, mashed, fresh peaches	4 lb
Dried chopped peaches	1½ lb
Sugar	2½ lb
Depectinizer	½ oz
Water	1 gallon
Yeast: Chablis or Hock	
Nutrient	

Method B. Aerobic fermentation five days. For a
sweet wine increase sugar to 3½ lb and substitute a
Sauterne yeast.

Pea pod   Believe it or not, pea pods make an attractive white
wine. Light in body, it is a wine that can be drunk
throughout the day.

Pea Pod wine (*medium*)

Chopped pea pods	4½ lb
Sugar	3 lb
Citric acid	½ oz
Tannin	¼ teaspoon
Water	1 gallon
Yeast: Zeltinger or Pommard	
Nutrient	

Method C. Aerobic fermentation four days. For a dry wine reduce the sugar to 2½ lb and increase tannin to ½ teaspoon. For a sweet wine increase sugar to 3½ lb and omit tannin.

Pear   Produces a wine that is extremely light, being low in both flavour and body. Pear is more often used in combination with other ingredients—but first try it on its own.

Pear wine (*medium*)

Minced pears	4 lb
Sugar	2¾ lb
Citric acid	½ oz
Campden tablet	1
Water	1 gallon
Yeast: Reisling	
Nutrient	

Method A. Aerobic fermentation four days.

Pearson Square See *Fortification*.

Pectin   This is a substance that occurs to a certain extent in all fruits. It is responsible for jam setting to a suitable consistency and for this reason is sometimes added to jams that are deficient. However, the winemaker has the opposite problem and if pectin is present in the finished wine a haze will occur. This can be prevented by the addition of depectinizer (see *Pectolase*) to musts that are particularly rich in pectin.

Fresh fruits that have a high pectin content are:

Black currants
Crab-apples
Damsons
Gooseberries
Grapefruit
Loganberries
Oranges
Peaches
Plums
Pineapple
Raspberries
Red currants
Sloes

Pectolase   More commonly called Depectinizer, pectolase is actually an enzyme. It acts upon the pectin and changes it to galacturonic acid or its methyl ester. This results in a clear wine that might otherwise be hazy.

Pectolase is best added before fermentation. If you are in doubt about a particular fruit you know little about regarding its pectin content—then add depectinizer to be on the safe side. If used, at least twenty-four hours should elapse before the yeast is added.

Peel   Here I am really talking about peel such as of orange, lemon and lime rather than apple, pear, etc., which is more properly called skin.

The pith (the fleshy white inner part) of the peel contains very bitter substances that will ruin a wine and is best avoided. However, the exterior part contains essential oils of the fruit and if a small portion is grated lightly into the must a wine will end up tasting like the parent fruit. This is strange but true; a wine made from orange juice will not end up with an orange taste—but it will if a little of the exterior peel is in the must.

Perry   Like Cider, Perry is made from the fruit only, with

	no added sugar. In this case the fruit is pear. Basically, therefore, it is really a low alcohol wine.
pH	This is a logarithmic scale that runs from 0 to 14 and provides a means of indicating the acidity or alkalinity of a liquid. The neutral point is pH 7. Below this, down to pH 0, the liquid is progressively more acid. Above this the acid content decreases until, at pH 14, an alkaline state exists with no acid present. The important point to remember is that a change in one pH unit represents a change of ten times the acid or alkaline concentration.
Phosphate	This in fact is an essential if the fermentation is to proceed. There is usually sufficient phosphate present in a fruit juice, but if for some reason it is lacking the fermentation will stop or 'stick'. In this case a small ($\frac{1}{2}$ teaspoon) amount of ammonium phosphate B.P. in each gallon of wine followed by a vigorous shaking or stirring will invariably get things going again.

As ammonium phosphate also contains nitrogen, it can be added to the must in place of ammonium sulphate.

Phylloxera	An aphid, or grape louse, the phylloxera devastated European vineyards. Commencing around 1860, the next fifty years saw virtually every vine in Europe destroyed. It was found that by grafting European wine stock on to the heavier, tougher, American vine roots a vine would survive. To this day, all European vines are growing on American roots, truly a case of trans-Atlantic co-operation!
Pineapple	Makes a very good white wine. As the juice is more easily, and just as cheaply, made into wine than either the fresh or canned fruit, I have given the recipe for that. Make sure that the juice is comprised of only fruit juice and sugar with no preservatives or artificial sweeteners.

Pineapple wine (medium)

Pineapple juice	2 pints
Sugar	$2\frac{1}{2}$ lb

Depectinizer	$\frac{1}{4}$ oz
Citric acid	$\frac{1}{4}$ oz
Tannin	$\frac{1}{2}$ teaspoon
Water up to	1 gallon

Yeast: Pommard or Chablis
Nutrient

Method A. Place in fermentation jar and fit air lock as soon as fermentation commences.

Plastics

This material has provided cheap, useful items of equipment and containers for the winemaker. But there are some dangers. Plastic containers in particular should be of a high-density plastic—the soft, cheap, low-density material will often taint the wine. In any case plastic should be completely sterilized before use. Even with top-grade high-density plastic, wine should be placed in a plastic container only as a temporary measure, say for must preparation and/or initial aerobic fermentation, but never for storage.

Plum

An excellent fruit for wine. Like damson the plum is rich in pectin and must be treated for this. For my own preference I use a Bordeaux yeast for a dry Plum wine, a Burgundy for medium and a Port for sweet.

Plum wine (dry)

Stoned, mashed plums	4 lb
Sugar	$2\frac{1}{2}$ lb
Depectinizer	$\frac{1}{2}$ oz
Water	1 gallon

Yeast: Bordeaux, Burgundy or Port
Nutrient

Method B. Aerobic fermentation five days.

Poisonous plants

Very little exhaustive research has gone into this subject and I doubt whether there is a really comprehensive list of fruits and plants that are poisonous for winemaking. However, here are some that are—or are reputed to be—poisonous: deadly nightshade, foxglove, most mushrooms, green potatoes, lobelia, lupins, mistletoe, laburnum, poppy, rhubarb leaves, thorn apple, wood anemone, woody nightshade, yew. The golden rule is the same as when picking wild mushrooms—if you don't know what it is, or you have never tried it, leave it alone.

Pomegranate   See Section Three.

Port   See Section Three.

Potassium hydrogen tartrate   It is this that sometimes falls to the bottom of wine in the form of crystals when tartaric acid has been present in the must. (See *Acid, Tartaric*.)

Potassium sorbate   A chemical used to prevent further fermentation when a wine is sweet but unfortified. It is added at the rate of 1·0 gm per gallon.

Potato   I am always puzzled when I see a wine labelled 'Potato'. A wine made solely from potatoes is a frightful, insipid thing. Wines bearing the name usually have additions such as raisin, ginger, lemon peel, etc., added, and it is these additions, and not the potato, which give the flavour. Moreover, many winemakers swear that some potatoes—especially green ones—can produce a poisonous liquid. Honestly, I am all for experiment, but potato is just not worth the bother!

Press   This is a device for extracting the maximum amount of juice from the fruit or pulp. Unless you are making considerable quantities a press is of no real value. But if you are contemplating something more ambitious, it is ideal—especially if you are making wine from something like grapes.

A word of warning. You might come across a press that was not designed specifically for winemaking. Fine. But make sure there are no metal parts such as iron or copper, or galvanized ware—or even lead!

Pressure cooker   This utilizes a more sophisticated method than just boiling. It will certainly sterilize fruit completely and reduce it to a suitable pulp. However, some fruits such as apples do seem to get a slightly 'cooked' flavour which is carried over into the wine; but hardier fruits such as elderberry hardly suffer at all.

Fruit and water are placed in the cooker, and the pressure raised to 15 lb/sq. in. for about ten minutes.

This method is definitely not suitable for most dried fruits, as a haze often occurs; or for flower wines, whose flavour is destroyed.

Primrose   Or more correctly, Primula Vulgaris. A very nice garden flower that also makes a useful wine.

Primrose wine (*medium*)

Primrose flowers	1 gallon
Sugar	3 lb
Citric acid	½ oz
Tannin	¼ teaspoon
Campden tablet	1
Water	1 gallon
Yeast: All Purpose	
Nutrient	

Method A. Aerobic fermentation four days.

Proof   A system of measuring and expressing the alcoholic content of a liquid. In the UK the Sikes scale is used, which means that at 60°F proof spirit contains 57·1 per cent by volume of alcohol; and 100 per cent spirit is 175·2 proof. In the USA proof is the double of alcoholic content by volume at 60°F and 100 per cent spirit in this case would be 200 proof.

It is really best to forget all this nonsense. The winemaker, clever chap, cuts all the corners by merely expressing his wine in simple proportions such as '12 per cent alcohol'.

Protein   A very complex chemical structure. Sometimes wine with a high proportion of fruit, if not properly matured, gives off a fine protein haze. This will sometimes fall clear if the wine is placed in a refrigerator for a few days. If this does not do the trick, a *Beutonite* treatment should clear it.

Prune   A much-maligned dried fruit, but an excellent wine. Use the recipe and method as for *Currant wine*, but substitute 4 lb minced stoned prunes for the currants and use a Tokay yeast.

Pump   A method of filtration by means of a suction pump which draws the wine through a fine paper filter. It is sometimes used for commercial wines but is generally too laborious for the amateur.

Pumpkin   For a long time pumpkin was considered rather a doubtful ingredient, producing a nasty-tasting wine. There is no doubt that this is not true, and I have made several excellent batches according to the recipe below.

Pumpkin wine (sweet)

Grated pumpkin flesh	5 lb
Sugar	$3\frac{1}{2}$ lb
Citric acid	$\frac{1}{2}$ oz
Water	1 gallon
Yeast: Hock	
Nutrient	

Method B. Aerobic fermentation three days.

Pyment   Any wine made from grapes and sweetened with honey.

Q

Quince   The Victorians believed that no apple tart was complete without a quince. It is now out of favour although it is quite popular in Spain for jams, etc. It makes a useful wine.

Quince wine (medium)

Pulped quinces	4 lb
Sugar	3 lb
Citric acid	$\frac{1}{2}$ oz
Depectinizer	$\frac{1}{2}$ oz
Water	1 gallon

Yeast: Chablis or Pommard
Nutrient

Method B. Aerobic fermentation four days.

Note: The above does not necessarily apply to the ornamental quince, which I have never tried.

R

Racking

This is the process of transferring clear or clearing wine from containers in which there is lees or sediment into clean containers. It is usually performed with the aid of a siphon tube, taking care to keep the

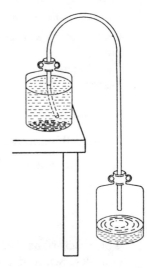

intake end clear of the bottom sediment. This is always done at least once. Even if the wine is brilliant and the lees firm at the bottom, one should always rack to avoid *Autolysis*.

Raisin

This of course is just dried grape, and although it will not make a wine identical to that made from fresh grape—it has a different character—it is every bit as good. Raisin is also one of the best ingredients to add to that recipe of yours which is just a bit lacking. If you do add it to other wines, remember that raisin contains approximately 50 per cent natural sugar.

Raisin wine (*medium*)

Minced raisins	6 lb
Citric acid	$\frac{1}{2}$ oz
Campden tablet	1
Water	1 gallon
Yeast: Burgundy or Bodeaux	
Nutrient	

Method B. Aerobic fermentation four days.

Raspberry — One of the few fruits that carry their natural flavour over into the wine. For this reason it is usually made sweet, but it makes an excellent, if unusual, dry wine. Use the recipe and method as for *Blackberry wine*.

Recipes — If you keep a log-book, recipe details will look after themselves. However, your favourite recipes will crop up with greater frequency in your log-book, making it a laborious job to look up the rare wine you made two years ago. And if a friend should give you his favourite recipe, you will need a safe place for it. So keep a recipe book in addition to a log-book.

Records — See *Log-books*.

Red Currant — See *Currant*.

Refrigeration — This method is used for grape wine so that tartrate crystals will be thrown out. Also, yeast will keep for a longer time if it is refrigerated. By refrigeration, I mean keeping a product cold, not freezing it solid.

Residual sugar — Should a wine contain any sugar—whether because the limit of alcohol tolerance has been reached, or because alcohol or stabilizers have been added—the remaining sweetness is termed the residual sugar.

Rhubarb — This is a difficult one. The bulk of rhubarb juice is high in oxalic acid, and this is very difficult to remove if the juice is heated. While many winemakers remove the acid by the addition of precipitated chalk, this affects the flavour, producing a rather flat, insipid wine. A better way is to dilute the oxalic acid —which is very sharp—and the following is the method and recipe I recommend.

Rhubarb wine (medium)

Chopped rhubarb	3 lb
Sugar	3 lb
Water	1 gallon

Yeast: Malaga or Tokay
Nutrient

Into a basin place a layer of chopped rhubarb, cover with sugar, another layer of rhubarb and so on. Leave for two days, then run off the juice, add enough water to clear the rhubarb of the rest of the sugar, run this off, then throw the rhubarb away. Do *not* squeeze or pulp it. Place the must in a fermentation jar with the rest of the sugar, add the yeast and cover the top with a cloth. When fermentation starts fit an air lock.

Rice   See *Sake.*
Ropiness   See *Mousiness.*
Rosé   Any very light red wine (light, in this case, meaning density of colour).
Rose hip   The Germans say that this is the next best thing to the grape for winemaking. If you have access to hedgerows or a large garden, the ingredients are free, except for the sugar.

Rose Hip wine (dry)

Fresh rose hips	3 lb
Dried rose hips	12 oz
Sugar	2½ lb
Citric acid	½ oz
Water	1 gallon

Yeast: Tokay or Reisling
Nutrient

Mince the rose hips. Method B. Aerobic fermentation four days.

Rosemary
A very strong herb. Although rosemary is sometimes used in combination with other ingredients, it does not make a decent wine on its own. In any case, whatever the recipe the rosemary leaves should not exceed 1 oz to the gallon of water.

Rose petal
Rose petals make a glorious, unusual wine—but only if made from the scented varieties. The petals without scent are no use.

Rose Petal wine (medium)

Rose petals	$\frac{1}{2}$ gallon
Sugar	3 lb
Citric acid	$\frac{1}{2}$ oz
Water	1 gallon
Yeast: Chablis or Champagne	
Nutrient	

Method B. Aerobic fermentation six days.

Rough
Description of a wine that has a harshness due to youth and immaturity. (See also *Astringency*.)

Rowanberry
See *Mountain Ash*.

Rubber
Most used perhaps in the form of a siphon tube or rubber bung. As a bung, in particular, it is vastly superior to a cork because rubber has better sealing qualities. This particularly applies to a 'drilled' bung for air lock fitting. Wine should not be kept in contact with rubber for any length of time.

S

Saccharin
An artificial sweetener. Like most artificial sweeteners, yeast will not convert it to alcohol during fermentation—so if there is any in the must the wine will be proportionately sweet after completion.

Sack
See Section Three.

Sage   Sometimes added to a recipe, sage does not make a good wine on its own.

Sake   Rice wine. The national Japanese drink. Rice wine, or Sake, please note, is made from rice *only*. Most recipes include raisins, grape concentrate or other additions. That is not the way to make Sake.

Sake, or Rice wine (dry)

Unpolished rice	1½ lb
Sugar	2½ lb
Citric acid	½ oz
Tannin	½ teaspoon
Water	1 gallon
Yeast: Cereal	
Nutrient	

Boil the rice until soft. Let the water cool, then proceed with method A. Aerobic fermentation six days.

Sarsaparilla   More frequently made into cordials, sarsaparilla makes a rather intriguing wine.

Sarsaparilla wine (sweet)

Chopped sarsaparilla leaves	1½ lb
Sugar	3½ lb
Citric acid	½ oz
Water	1 gallon
Yeast: All Purpose	
Nutrient	

Method B. Aerobic fermentation five days.

Seals   See *Corks*.
Sherry   See Section Three.
Sinker   A perforated board or grid which holds the ingredients in the must under the surface. This avoids a *Cap* forming and to a certain extent reduces the chances of bacterial contamination.

Siphon   A tube for racking wine from one container into another.

Sloe High in acid, pectin and tannin, sloes make an excellent wine. But be sure they are very ripe.

Sloe wine (medium)

Crushed ripe sloes	3 lb
Sugar	3 lb
Depectinizer	½ oz
Campden tablet	1
Water	1 gallon
Yeast: Burgundy	
Nutrient	

Method A. Aerobic fermentation—two days if the wine is to be drunk soon after bottling, or five days if you can leave it for a year or two. The latter produces a superb wine. For a dry wine reduce the sugar to 2½ lb and substitute a Bordeaux yeast.

Sodium meta-bisulphite This is sometimes added to fruit pulp at the rate of 1 gm to the gallon of must, to prevent browning of light-coloured juices and to guard against bacterial infection.

Sparkling wine See *Champagne*, Section Three.

Specific gravity This is the principle which the hydrometer uses to assess the density of the must or wine. In this case, the greater the sugar content the thicker, or denser, the liquid will be; the lower the sugar content, and the higher the alcohol content, the thinner it will be. Distilled water, at a temperature of 59°F, is given an arbitrary specific gravity of 1·000. Thus any figure higher than this, e.g. 1·088 SG, indicates that there is sugar present. A lower reading, e.g. 0·980 SG, indicates that not only is there no sugar present but also that the alcohol content is above average. (See also *Hydrometer* and *Strength*.)

Spice In the form of ginger, clove, cinnamon, etc., has been used for hundreds of years for flavouring wines. The usual way is to add a small portion to the must, but the spice(s) can be placed in a small linen bag and hung in the fermenting must until the required flavour is reached. As with most 'additives' it must be borne in mind that a spice—or, indeed, the wine itself—will not have the same smell or flavour during a lengthy period of storing. If a wine is flavoured with, say, cinnamon, the wine when new will have a flavour and aroma of cinnamon. But after a year or two there will be a bouquet and flavour that will be entirely different. You may prefer it, or not, but you must bear it in mind.

Squash

From the same family as the marrow, but it makes a better wine. Use the recipe and method as for *Marrow*, but it is better to use white sugar instead of brown.

Stabilizing

A wine is said to be stable when there is no danger of further fermentation. Several rackings will contribute to stability—but this method is by no means certain. One certain way is to fortify your wine with spirit—but this will produce a wine too strong for the table. The best and most certain method for our purpose is to add an element that will effectively prevent any further fermentation. One gramme of potassium sorbate can be added for each gallon of wine. Or use any of the many proprietary wine stabilizers on the market.

Starch

Present in fruits such as apple, banana and, of course, ingredients such as oats and other cereals. When using such ingredients it is often advisable to use a special yeast that attacks starch. This is usually marketed as Cereal Yeast. Starch can sometimes be the cause of a haze (see *Iodine solution*).

Starter

When a yeast is added to a must, it sometimes takes several days for fermentation to start. This is caused by several things: the dilution of the yeast in the bulk, the difficulty of keeping a considerable quantity of wine at the correct temperature, etc. The way to ensure that a fermentation will start immediately is to prepare a 'starter bottle'. This is a bottle of liquid in full ferment that is added to the must. The yeast then will commence work immediately. The starter, of course, must be made forty-eight hours before you start your wine, so that it will be fermenting fully, and is made from the juice of the fruit to be used and the intended yeast. Or you can make one up with a tablespoonful of granulated sugar, the juice of a lemon (or a pinch of citric acid), and a half pint of water. Keep in a warm (75°F) place until fermentation starts. The starter bottle can then be kept in a suitably warm place (it is easier to do this with a half-pint bottle than your one- or five-gallon container!) until fermentation starts and is ready to be added to the must.

Steam
Often used for sterilizing ingredients and/or equipment. It is really a rather cumbersome method for the amateur, who is better off using methods such as sulphiting.

Sterilization
This can be achieved for equipment by means of steam, heat or chemicals, and it is the latter that should be used by the amateur. The most common and effective method is to prepare a sterilizing liquid that can be stored for use when required. To prepare a 1 per cent sulphite solution add 2½ oz of sodium metabisulphite to 1 gallon of water (or proportionately). This can be used to rinse bottles and swab or rinse equipment.

Sticking
Sometimes a fermentation will stop or 'stick' before all the sugar has been converted. This might be because too much sugar has been added at the beginning and the yeast has reached the limit of alcohol tolerance. In this case dilution with the same juice, or even plain water, might start things up again. Alternatively, if the temperature of the ferment has been too high the yeast might have been killed, or halted because of too low a temperature. The cause could also be insufficient oxygen, or too much carbon dioxide. In the case of either the wine should be aerated by pouring (not racking) from one container to another. (See also *Thiamine*.)

Storing wine
See *Cellar*.

Straining   See *Filtration*.

Strawberry   Makes a really fine wine. As with Raspberry, the flavour of the fruit comes through to the finished wine. For this reason Strawberry wine is often made sweet and used as a dessert wine, and although it is excellent in this capacity, I like to make a quantity of dry Strawberry wine for casual drinking. Served cold on a hot summer's day it is quite superb.

Strawberry wine (dry)

Mashed strawberries	4 lb
Sugar	$2\frac{1}{2}$ lb
Depectinizer	$\frac{1}{2}$ oz
Campden tablet	1
Water	1 gallon
Yeast: Sauterne	
Nutrient	

Method A. Aerobic fermentation one day. For a sweet wine increase sugar to $3\frac{1}{2}$ lb.

Strength   This is really the alcohol content of the wine, a 'strong' wine being one that is high in alcohol. (See also *Alcohol, Hydrometer, Proof, Specific gravity*.)

A lot is made about the strength of wine, but many winemakers are not aware that, even using a hydrometer, the strength of your wine can be assessed only *approximately*. This is because of a variety of circumstances, including the amount of time of aerobic fermentation, temperature variations when using the hydrometer and many other errors that can accumulate. This means that the hydrometer method, although invaluable in many respects, is still an indirect method of assessing alcoholic strength of a finished wine.

The only accurate way of gauging alcoholic strength is by means of a wine refractometer. This requires knowledge of its use, and in addition it is something like one hundred times more expensive than a hydrometer! Because of its complexity and expense the wine refractometer has not been included in this book.

Sugar Most sugars can be used for the production of wine, the most popular being white granulated; this has the advantage of being comparatively neutral in flavour and colour. Brown sugar on the other hand has a pronounced flavour and gives the wine a golden tinge. Demerara sugar gives even more flavour and colour. This is not to say that brown and demerara are unsuitable—they are in fact very useful for ingredients that are lacking in character. (See also *Invert sugar*.)

Sugar beet See *Beet sugar*.

Sulphite See *Sulphur*.

Sulphur The burning of sulphur in wine casks to keep the interior free from bacteria has been used for centuries. This burning produces a gas which is present in certain amounts as a salt in Campden tablets. So when we 'sulphite' our wines or equipment by means of Campden tablets we are not using new-fangled chemical compounds but a principle that has been proved by winemakers over the centuries.

Sultana Makes an excellent golden wine. Use the recipe and method as for *Raisin wine*, but substitute a Chablis or Sauterne yeast.

Sunlight See *Light*.

T

Table wine A wine suitable for drinking with a meal. This does not denote the degree of sweetness, because, while a dry wine is invariably the most suitable for the primary and main courses, a sweeter wine is often the most suitable with dessert.

Taints Off flavours that the wine might pick up in production. This can be caused by metal contamination, particularly copper, or by bad technique such as occurs with autolysis—which is the fault of the wine-maker.

Tangerine Makes an excellent white wine. Use the recipe and method as for *Orange wine*.

Tannin Present in the skins of most fruits. Tannin, in excess, makes a wine very astringent, which requires extensive ageing. On the other hand, if tannin is absent the wine lacks bite. Where a fruit is rich in tannin, nothing need be added, but for fruit that is lacking, and for flower, root and cereal wines, a small quantity of tannin will vastly improve the taste, adding a little bite or zest. This is particularly necessary with dry wines.

Tansy A herb that is used to add bitterness to wines. It should be added in very small quantities—boil up a small measure in a pint of water and try this out in a small quantity of wine first.

Taps Where taps are fitted to casks or other containers, they should be completely dismantled, washed and sterilized before use or when changing from one wine to another.

Tasting This can be a very simple 'I like it or I don't' assessment or a complex art of judgment.

Wine tasting has its own jargon (aroma, bouquet, etc.) that, once learnt, is quite precise and well worth learning. When tasting or judging a wine external influences must be taken into account. Take two bottles of the same wine and drink one with, say, steak one day and with jugged hare the next. They will taste like different wines. So if you are tasting purely for the sake of judging or assessing, make sure the external influences are always the same. If I am tasting I partake of nothing but plain white bread and water between sips of wine. Some of my friends swear by mild cheese. It does not really matter as long as you always do the same thing.

Tea Usually added to dried fruit wines, tea can be an attractive wine in its own right. You can experiment with various types of Indian and China teas.

Tea wine (dry)

Tea	2 oz
Sugar	2½ lb
Citric acid	½ oz
Water	1 gallon

Yeast: Bordeaux
Nutrient

Pour 4 pints of the water, boiling, over the tea. Infuse for half an hour. Strain into the rest of the water. Method A. As soon as fermentation commences place in fermentation jar and fit air lock.

Temperature   One of the most important aspects of *Fermentation*. (See also Section One, p.18.)

Thermometer   An important item of winemaking equipment, because the temperature of the *Fermentation* is often critical.

Thiamine   This is vitamin B, and is useful when sticking occurs as it increases the activity of the yeast. A small pinch is enough for a gallon of wine.

Tinned fruit   See *Canned food*.

Tomato   This makes a wine that does not appeal to me, but don't let this prevent you from trying it—many of my friends find it quite enjoyable.

Tomato wine (dry)

Squashed ripe tomatoes	6 lb
Sugar	2½ lb
Citric acid	½ oz
Depectinizer	½ oz
Campden tablet	1
Water	1 gallon

Yeast: All Purpose
Nutrient

Method B. Aerobic fermentation four days.

Topping up   This is done to a fermentation jar after the first vigorous fermentation. The jar is filled or topped up to within an inch or two of the air lock by means of a

liquid made to the same strength as the original must.

Torula   One of the bacteria which causes *Oiliness*.

Turnip   Makes a wine similar to, but not as good as, Parsnip. Use the recipe and method as for *Parsnip wine*.

V

Vanilla   Used as a flavouring. (See *Spice*.)

Vegetable   Most vegetables can be made to produce an acceptable wine (see under respective headings). They are invariably deficient in balancing ingredients such as tannin, acid and essentials such as sugar, and where necessary these have to be added.

Veitch berry   This is a cross between a blackberry and the raspberry November Abundance. Makes a very good wine. Use the recipe and method as for *Blackberry wine*.

Ventilation   This really relates to the storing of wine. Dampness, condensation and moulds are all enemies of the cork. It will also wreak havoc with labels and any wood items such as barrels. Always ensure that the place you store your wine in is suitably ventilated without causing draughts.

Vine   The plant of the grape.

Vinegar   The bane of the winemaker. Vinegar is the undesirable result of the bacteria *Acetobacter*.

Vin ordinaire   'Ordinaire' is French for common or ordinary. It broadly defines an unpretentious wine for everyday drinking.

Vintage   In wine terms this is more usually applied to grape wines, although there is no reason why it should not apply to any other. If the term is used, it must be remembered that the vintage date is the year of the harvesting or growing and *not* the date when the wine is actually made or bottled.

Vitamins   See *Thiamine*.

W

Wallflower One of the more delicate flower wines. Make sure the flowers are freshly picked or the wine may develop some 'off' flavours.

Wallflower wine (medium)

Wallflower blossoms	½ gallon
Sugar	3 lb
Citric acid	½ oz
Tannin	pinch
Water	1 gallon
Yeast: Hock	
Nutrient	

Method A. Aerobic fermentation four days.

Walnut leaf The same applies to this as to oak leaves. Use the recipe and method as for *Oak Leaf wine*.

Wassail bowl A very ancient drink that varies slightly according to locality. The principal ingredients are Sherry and beer, flavoured with a variety of spices.

Water Perhaps the most overlooked and underestimated ingredient in winemaking. It is often forgotten that the bulk of the most delectable wine consists of water.

It is essential that the water used in winemaking is free from impurities, bacteria and taints, for these can impart disease and odd flavours to the wine. While most tap water is sufficiently pure for our purpose, if possible boil it to kill any bacteria.

Waxing Sometimes used on corks to enhance their sealing qualities, or on the inside of wooden wine barrels for the same reason.

A good cork will require nothing to help it seal correctly—but a cheap cork might and you should not use one of these. As for the wooden barrels, several costly experiments have been carried out on the Continent using this method, and while it has now achieved a degree of success, it is too much of a gamble for the amateur winemaker.

Wheat	Makes an excellent neutral wine. Use the recipe and method as for *Barley wine*.
Whin	This is the common gorse or furze. It makes an agreeable but not very distinctive wine. Use the recipe and method as for *Broom wine*.
White currant	See *Currant*.
Whortleberry	A local name for *Bilberry*.
Wild yeast	See *Yeast* and *Kloeckera apiculatus*.
Wine	The 'Concise Oxford Dictionary' defines wine as 'fermented grape juice' or 'fermented drink resembling wine made from specified fruit, etc.'. This would indicate that wine is *only* from grape juice; all others bearing only a *resemblance*.
	While one would hesitate to argue with the 'C.O.D.', there is room for argument. Grape has been the accepted juice from time immemorial only because it is the easiest fruit to make wine from. Just squash it, leave it and you have wine! Most other fruits need additions to the must to make a suitable wine and, if this is the criterion of true wine, it must be said here and now that the noble grape is sometimes deficient in this respect. It is not unknown for some excellent commercial winemakers to resort to adding a 'syrup' of sugar and water to the must after a poor year's weather. The ordinary type of grape eaten in the house is no more suitable for wine than, say, plums. Wine grapes are a special breed.
Wineberry	A species of raspberry. Use the recipe and method as for *Blackberry wine*.
Wiring	This is carried out with sparkling wine to secure the corks and stop them from flying out under the internal pressure. The job is best done with proper wire loops and a hand wiring tool.
Wood	In winemaking this usually refers to *Barrels*, but there are various items of equipment that are often of wood. It must be borne in mind that wood, being relatively absorbent, is prone to carry bacteria and should be regularly sterilized.
Woodruff	A spring plant with small, white, starry flowers.

It is a good old-fashioned favourite that is well worth making if you can find enough among the leaf-mould of beech woods. Officially it is of the order Rubinacae. Use the recipe and method as for *Burnet wine.*

Y

Yarrow Or Milfoil. Makes a reasonable but not exciting wine. Use the recipe and method as for *Broom wine.*

Yeast Microscopic botanical cells that secrete enzymes, causing fermentation by the conversion of sugar into alcohol and carbon dioxide.

There are many varieties of yeast and it functions best under certain circumstances (see *Enzymes* and *Fermentation*). It also comes in various forms. Bakers yeast is almost a thick paste and, while suitable for the rank amateur, is not quite suitable for the production of really good wine because it is intended, primarily, for the production of bread, not wine. This is even more true of brewers yeast, which is suitable only for beer and ale. Dried and liquid yeasts are also sold and they are admirable as long as the yeast variety is suitable.

Whenever possible, use a dried or liquid wine yeast. This is derived from the skins of fruit specific to a locality which are bred for greater 'stamina' than the *Wild yeasts*—these have a limited alcohol tolerance and are inclined to give off flavours. (See also *Agar.*)

Section Three

Imitating commercial wines.

Exotic or unusual wines.

Ancient recipes from early writers.

This is really a three-part section designed to whet the appetite of the winemaker and to prove that the craft has more to offer than the production of a wine from the most available ingredients.

The first part explains how you can make wines very similar to the commercial varieties, from quite common fruit. The second lists some wines made from unusual fruits such as guava and mango, so that not only will you have excellent wines but also a subject for conversation! Finally, you will find some recipes from old books that go back, in some cases, more than two hundred years.

Imitating commercial wines

Home winemakers—particularly the Germans—have been having increased success in the quest to produce wines similar to some commercial varieties from various ingredients. Here is a list of recipes that you might like to try. With care you should be able to confound your friends and satisfy your palate.

Beaujolais

Beaujolais style

Fresh, crushed elderberries	3 lb
Minced raisins	3 lb
Sugar	1 lb
Campden tablet	1
Water	1 gallon
Yeast: Beaujolais	
Nutrient	

Method B: Aerobic fermentation four days.

Burgundy   *Burgundy style*

Dried bilberries	12 oz
Minced raisins	8 oz
Sugar	2½ lb
Tartaric acid	¼ oz
Water	1 gallon
Yeast: Burgundy	
Nutrient	

Method B. Aerobic fermentation five days.

Chablis   *Chablis style*

Crushed green gooseberries	2 lb
White grape concentrate	1 pint
Sugar	1 lb
Depectinizer	½ oz
Campden tablet	1
Water up to	1 gallon
Yeast: Chablis	
Nutrient	

Method B. Aerobic fermentation three days.

Champagne   I was originally keen to add Champagne to this list
of recipes. However, a couple of incidents have
persuaded me that this might be unwise. Champagne
is a sparkling wine, and as such a considerable
pressure is built up inside the bottle as a result of
those little bubbles. I had always considered that
the danger of exploding bottles was non-existent if
care and proper Champagne bottles were used. But
I have recently heard of two separate cases in which
experienced winemakers have had bottles explode.
Luckily no one was around to get hurt—but there
could have been, so I am not including the recipe.

If it is any consolation, expert wine tasters often
'swizzle' the bubbles out of Champagne if they are
tasting. They say the actual wine cannot be tasted
properly while it is fizzing; so, if it spoils the taste,
why put them in?

Chianti

Chianti style

Crushed fresh elderberries	4 lb
Peeled mashed bananas	1 lb
Red grape concentrate	1 pint
Sugar	1 lb
Campden tablet	1
Depectinizer	$\frac{1}{2}$ oz
Water up to	1 gallon
Yeast: Chianti	
Nutrient	

Method C, but add concentrate after the must has cooled. Aerobic fermentation only one day.

Claret

This applies to the wines of the Bordeaux region, and there are many types of dry red wine for which the area is justly famed. The following recipe, with care, will provide you with a good approximation of good Claret—and in any case makes a superb red wine in its own right.

Claret style

Dried elderberries	$\frac{1}{2}$ lb
Minced raisins	1 lb
Sugar	2 lb
Tartaric acid	$\frac{1}{4}$ oz
Water	1 gallon
Yeast: Bordeaux	
Nutrient	

Method B. Aerobic fermentation six days.

Hock

Hock style

Crushed green gooseberries	4 lb
Minced sultanas	1 lb
White grape concentrate	$\frac{1}{2}$ pint
Rose petals	$\frac{1}{2}$ pint
Sugar	1 lb
Depectinizer	$\frac{1}{2}$ oz
Campden tablet	1

Water to   1 gallon
Yeast: Hock
Nutrient

Method A. Aerobic fermentation four days.

Madeira   See also *Estufa* in Section Two. Madeira is really a process of treating a wine. Madeira itself consists of five different types of wine ranging from sweet to dry—so it would be impossible to emulate it in a single recipe. Further, each Madeira wine is treated in an 'estufa', which means that it is subjected to a degree of heat for a specified period of time. During this process it acquires an intriguing flavour which appeals to many people.

It is comparatively easy for some homes to try this method for their wines. What you need is a place where your wine can be kept at a specified, relatively constant temperature. Madeira, like Port or Sherry, is a fortified wine, so you will have to add some spirit to an ordinary table wine (see the Pearson Square in *Fortification*, Section Two) to obtain a wine approximately 20 per cent alcohol by volume. Try it on one of your wines. One point though—after treatment your 'estufa' wine will require at least several months in bottle to benefit properly.

The temperatures used vary proportionately with the time taken and range from 130°F (54°C) for three months for the cheapest wines to 90°F (32°C) for nine months for the very best wines.

Port   This is a fortified wine that has spirit added before fermentation is completed. The spirit ensures that the yeast is killed and the remaining sugar adds a richness that some people are fond of and others dislike.

You will have to achieve an alcohol content of approximately 20 per cent by volume, and the wine-maker can do this in two ways. (1) By the addition of spirit (see the Pearson Square in *Fortification*, p. 69), which is expensive. (2) By getting the maximum alcoholic content out of the fermentation, which is much cheaper. This means that you must use a hydrometer. The sugar is added in stages, no more than 4 oz at a time for a gallon of must, during fermentation. Each time the hydrometer reading drops to zero, the next dose of sugar (in the form of a syrup) is added. This will ensure that you will get the maximum alcohol content before your yeast dies of exhaustion. When fermentation ceases, stop adding sugar. (See also *Hydrometer*, Section Two.)

Port style

Dried bilberries	2 lb
Mashed peeled bananas	1 lb
Red grape concentrate	1 pint
Depectinizer	$\frac{1}{2}$ oz
Sugar	$3\frac{1}{2}$ lb (approx.)
Water up to	1 gallon
Yeast: Port	
Nutrient	

Boil the bananas in the water for $\frac{1}{4}$ hour. Strain off, and pour the hot liquid over the bilberries. When cool proceed with method A. Aerobic fermentation six days.

Sherry

This is a fortified wine, spirit being added after fermentation has finished. As with *Port* the amateur winemaker has two ways of achieving the required alcohol content of around 20 per cent by volume. Sherry acquires its characteristics not only from the yeast but also from the soil in the Jerez region, which is rich in calcium sulphate (plaster of Paris). This is also added to the must of a dry Sherry. The sugar should be added as for the procedure for *Port*.

Sherry style (sweet)

Peeled mashed bananas	1 lb
Minced sultanas	2 lb
Chopped crab apples (or cooking)	1 lb

Crushed ripe gooseberries	1 lb
Sugar	3½ lb (approx.)
Tartaric acid	¼ oz
Depectinizer	¼ oz
Water up to	1 gallon
Yeast: Sherry	
Nutrient	

Boil the bananas in the water for ¼ hour. Strain off and pour the hot liquid over the sultanas, apples and gooseberries. When cool proceed as for method A. Aerobic fermentation four days.

Exotic or unusual wines

Artichoke A very nice dry wine that is made from the tubers of the Jerusalem artichoke (not the globe artichoke).

Artichoke wine (dry)

Washed, sliced artichoke tubers	4 lb
Sugar	2½ lb
Citric acid	½ oz
Tannin	½ teaspoon
Water	1 gallon
Yeast: Reisling	
Nutrient	

Method C. Aerobic fermentation four days.

Aubergine Makes a reasonable dry white wine. But make sure the aubergine is ripe; if it's not the wine will taste dreadfully woody.

Aubergine wine (dry)

Sliced aubergine	4 lb
Sugar	2½ lb
Citric acid	½ oz
Tannin	½ teaspoon
Water	1 gallon
Yeast: Zeltinger or Chablis	
Nutrient	

Method B. Aerobic fermentation three days.

Guava
This makes an elegant, attractive wine. It is a trifle expensive to make from fresh fruit so I have used a recipe for canned fruit.

Guava wine (medium)

One-pound tins guava halves	3
Sugar	$2\frac{1}{2}$ lb
Citric acid	$\frac{1}{2}$ oz
Tannin	$\frac{1}{2}$ teaspoon
Depectinizer	$\frac{1}{2}$ oz
Water up to	1 gallon
Yeast: Champagne	
Nutrient	

Method A. Aerobic fermentation four days.

Lychee
A really decisious white wine, dry or sweet.

Lychee wine (dry)

Lychees, stoned	5 lb
Sugar	$2\frac{1}{2}$ lb
Citric acid	$\frac{1}{4}$ oz
Tannin	$\frac{1}{2}$ teaspoon
Water up to	1 gallon
Yeast: Chablis	
Nutrient	

The lychees should be finely chopped. Method B. Aerobic fermentation five days.

Mango
A really nice unusual wine. Once again I have utilized canned fruit. Use the recipe and method as for *Guava wine* (above), but reduce the ingredients to two one-pound tins and omit the tannin.

Morat
A very popular Anglo-Saxon drink made from mulberries and honey. Use the recipe and method as for *Bilberry wine* (Section Two) but replace the sugar with $3\frac{1}{2}$ lb of honey.

Paw-paw   Produces an excellent dry white wine.

Paw-paw wine (dry)

One-pound tins paw-paw cubes	2
Sugar	2 lb
Citric acid	½ oz
Tannin	½ teaspoon
Campden tablet	1
Water up to	1 gallon

Yeast: Champagne
Nutrient

Method A. Aerobic fermentation five days.

Pomegranate   A delicious wine of unusual flavour. The skin and pips are high in tannin and it is best if the fruit itself is put in a press and the juice extracted. If peel or crushed pips are present the wine will be too astringent.

Pomegranate wine (medium)

Pomegranate juice	2 pints
Sugar	3 lb
Citric acid	¼ oz
Campden tablet	1
Water up to	1 gallon

Yeast: Pommard
Nutrient

Method A. Place in fermentation jar and fit air lock as soon as fermentation commences.

Ancient recipes

Although wine has been made for thousands of years, it is only comparatively recently that the reason for fermentation—yeast—was discovered. Consequently, old winemaking books have no mention of this essential ingredient. Moreover, their recipes were usually for enormous quantities, so I have been forced to do an editing job to present the recipes in a more modern format. I apologize to the original authors: but modern man in a tiny flat is not able to make his gooseberry wine in ten-gallon lots, and he is not inclined to resort to prayer to induce fermentation!

> Recipes from
> *The Complete Cook,*
> by James Jenks, 1768

Christmas Elderberry

Minced raisins (original recipe specifies Malaga or Lipari raisins)	4 lb
Dried elderberries	4 oz
Stoned damsons	1 lb
Sugar	$1\frac{1}{2}$ lb
Depectinizer	$\frac{1}{2}$ oz
Citric acid	$\frac{1}{4}$ oz
Campden tablet	1
Water	1 gallon
Yeast: All Purpose	
Nutrient	

Soak the raisins, elderberries, damsons and Campden tablet in the water for ten days, stirring every day, adding the depectinizer after eight days. Strain off and add the rest of the ingredients (with the yeast preferably as a starter bottle). Pour into fermentation jar and fit air lock as soon as fermentation commences.

English Sack or Saragosa

Rue	4 sprigs
Sliced fennel root	8 oz
Honey	3 lb
Water	1 gallon
Yeast: All Purpose	
Nutrient	

Boil the rue and fennel in the water for half an hour, adding the honey ten minutes from the end. Skim and strain. When cool add yeast and nutrient. Pour into fermentation jar and fit air lock as soon as fermentation commences.

Lemon Shrub

Brandy	2 pints
Lemon juice	½ pint
Lemon peel (no pith)	2 lemons
Sugar	1 lb

This, of course, is not a wine, but it is fun and an extremely old drink. It also makes the brandy slightly cheaper!

Place all the ingredients in a securely corked jar for twenty-four hours, shaking several times and ensuring that the sugar is completely dissolved. Remove or strain off the lemon peel and recork. Bottle after several months. To make Orange Shrub use orange juice and peel—in this case only ½ lb of sugar should be used.

Recipes from
A Treatise on Family Winemaking,
by P. P. Carnell, 1814

Quote from the text:

'The causes that produce the effects of vinous fermentation are imperfectly known, for no chemical exploration as yet has been able to discover but a few well-ascertained facts.'

Apple Red

Minced apples	15 lb
Sliced raw beetroot	2 lb
Ground ginger	1 oz
Rosemary leaves	¼ oz
Lavender leaves	½ pint
Sugar	3½ lb
Water	2 gallons
Yeast: All Purpose	
Nutrient	
Spirit*	2 pints

Boil the beetroot in the water until tender. While still boiling add the rest of the ingredients except yeast and nutrient, which is added when the must has cooled. Aerobic fermentation four days. Strain off into fermentation jar and fit air lock.

*In the recipe, two pints of spirit (unnamed) are added when fermentation has ceased. This, of course, is up to your discretion—it sounds an intriguing combination as it is!

Dutch and Currant

Red currants	5 lb
Sliced raw beetroot	$\frac{1}{2}$ lb
Ground ginger	$\frac{1}{2}$ oz
Ground bitter almonds	$\frac{1}{4}$ oz
Sugar	$2\frac{1}{2}$ lb
Water	1 gallon
Yeast: All Purpose	
Nutrient	
Brandy*	$\frac{1}{4}$ pint

Boil the beetroot in the water until tender. Add the currants, crushed, when you take it off the boil. Add the rest of the ingredients when cool. Aerobic fermentation four days.

*The brandy is part of the recipe and is added when the wine has finished fermenting. If you want to leave it out it would be better to increase the sugar to 3 lb.

Honey White

White currants	3 lb
Balm leaves	$\frac{1}{2}$ pint
Sweetbriar*	$\frac{1}{2}$ pint
Honey	$3\frac{1}{2}$ lb
Water	1 gallon
Yeast: All Purpose	
Nutrient	
Brandy	$\frac{1}{4}$ pint

Method as for previous recipe—*Dutch and Currant.*

*Sweetbriar (Rosa Eglanteria) is a sweetly scented type of wild rose. The petals are used. You could just as well use petals from a fragrant rose.

Recipes from
A Treatise on the Art of Making Wine from Native Fruits,
by Frederick Accum, 1820

Cowslip

Cowslip flowers	2 pints
Rinds of lemons (no pith)	12
Sugar	$1\frac{1}{2}$ lb
Water	
Yeast: Ale (brewers yeast)	
Nutrient	

Dissolve the sugar in the water and add all the ingredients. Aerobic fermentation six days.

In fact, the recipe states that the cowslips be added 'When the fermentation is nearly over'. This of course refers to a complete aerobic fermentation. It would be pointless to do this. Also, the sugar is rather meagre and will result in a weak wine; $2\frac{1}{2}$ lb would be a more sensible amount. I know that brewers yeast is not used by the modern winemaker, but ...!

Mixed Fruit

Stoned cherries	1 lb
Black currants	1 lb
White currants	1 lb
Raspberries	1 lb
Sugar	3 lb
Water	1 gallon
Yeast: All Purpose	
Nutrient	
Brandy	$\frac{1}{4}$ pint

Mash the fruit and steep for three days in the water. Strain through fine sieve pressing the pulp dry. Add the rest of the ingredients. When fermenting pour into fermentation jar and fit air lock.

The recipe states that the brandy should be added after two weeks' fermentation. Personally I would ferment the wine right out and forget the brandy.

Orange

Peel (no pith) and juice of oranges	10
Sugar	2½ lb
Water up to	1 gallon
Yeast: All Purpose	
Nutrient	

Bring half a gallon of water to the boil. Take off the heat and add the peel. Let stand overnight, strain off and add the juice. Bring volume up to 1 gallon. Add yeast and nutrient. When fermentation commences pour into fermentation jar and fit air lock.

Further Reading

Books

'Amateur Winemaker' Recipes, C. J. J. Berry, Amateur Winemaker

Making Wines Like Those You Buy, Acton and Duncan, Amateur Winemaker

Book of Home Wine Making and Brewing, B. C. A. Turner, Boots the Chemists

Scientific Winemaking—made easy, J. R. Mitchell, Amateur Winemaker

Amateur Winemaking, S. M. Tritton, Faber & Faber

Winemaker's Cookbook, Tilly Timbrell and Bryan Acton, Amateur Winemaker

Winemaking with Canned and Dried Fruit, C. J. J. Berry, Amateur Winemaker

Judging Home-made Wines, Amateur Winemaker

Magazines

The Amateur Winemaker

Home Beer and Winemaking